D1563847

# TRIDUUM

# A Triduum Sourcebook

# Acknowledgments

This book collects materials from numerous sources. We are grateful to these publishers and authors. Every effort has been made to determine the ownership of all texts and to make proper arrangements for their use. Any oversight that may have occurred, if brought to our attention, will gladly be corrected in future editions.

Acknowledgments for sources not listed below are in the endnotes.

Excerpts from the *Book of Common Prayer,* 1979, as published by the Church Hymnal Corporation, New York.

Excerpts from the English translation of the *Lectionary for Mass* © 1969, International Committee on English in the Liturgy, Inc. (ICEL); excerpts from the English translation of the *Roman Calendar* © 1970, ICEL; excerpts from the English translation of *The Roman Missal* © 1973, ICEL; excerpts from the English translation of the *Rite of Christian Initiation of Adults* © 1978, ICEL. All rights reserved.

Texts of psalms and canticles taken from *The Psalms: A New Translation* © 1963 The Grail (England). The complete psalms first published in 1963 by and available through William Collins Sons & Co. Ltd. All rights reserved.

Scripture readings are taken from the *Lectionary for Mass,* copyright © 1970, and the *New American Bible,* copyright © 1970, by the Confraternity of Christian Doctrine, Washington DC, and are used by license of copyright owner. All rights reserved.

Design by Michael Tapia

# A TRIDUUM SOURCEBOOK

*Edited by*
Gabe Huck
Mary Ann Simcoe

# Contents

# Introduction

From our ancestors we have received gestures, tunes, a calendar, a sense of good order—and words. From all of these our prayer is fashioned. Words by themselves are not prayer. But the words name our gestures, fill our tunes, give face and dearness to our calendar, keep modest place in our orders of service. Nothing in this book intends to disturb that proper modesty. Words will always serve best in prayer when they are loved and are in proportion to the moment.

What the church is doing on the paschal night cannot be found in a book, cannot be reduced to the words spoken and sung. Yet the words are what the tradition most generously preserves. This is a book of those words, words from and about the prayer of that night and of the Triduum which embraces it.

The words of the tradition and of the present liturgical books convey the intensity and unity of the hours around the Vigil. They presume and demand a church that is fasting and praying and keeping watch. For we are face to face now with that which runs beneath every life every day: the evil that is unwearied whether trivial or monstrous. We are face to face and therefore boldly exultant, and we fast now not in mortification but in delight. The Triduum is simply the time it takes us to gather at the font where we all began a lifelong passover. Our words are ever trying to express how hard and beautiful is this passing over that makes the church.

The words, then, are the scriptures of the Roman rite for the principal liturgies of Holy Thursday, Good Friday and the Vigil. They are most of the prayers from the sacramentary. Those involved in the preparation of liturgy and homily may thus choose to make this a workbook. But the scriptures and prayers are bound in with poems, hymns, preaching, fragments from other rites, contemporary reflections. More than a workbook, then, this is a companion for the Triduum, an unfolding of the paschal mystery, a prayerbook for the catechumen-becoming-neophyte and the long-baptized Christian alike.

The words this collection brings to the reader for a first time are worthy of familiarity; more important and more difficult, the familiar words are worthy of distance, fresh hearing, time. May all of them—in their various moods and meanings—give us a sense for the shape of these days and for their public rituals.

Thanks are due to those who responded to the concept of this book with suggestions for texts to be included: Agnes Cunningham, SSCM, Carl Dehne, SJ, Brian Helge, Mary McGann, RSCJ, Sam Mackintosh, Frank Quinn, OP, and Peter Scagnelli. Linda Murphy and Elizabeth-Anne Vanek composed prayers of intercession, and the service of paschal vespers is the work of Andrew Ciferni, Laurence Mayer and Alan Scheible. Suggestions came from many others. To all of them our thanks.

FOR our sake Christ was obedient, accepting
even death,
death on a cross.
Therefore God raised him on high
and gave him the name above all other names.

Philippians 2:8–9<br>Liturgy of the Hours<br>Roman rite

THE church does not pretend, as it were, that it does
not know what will happen with the crucified Jesus. It
does not sorrow and mourn over the Lord as if the church
itself were not the very creation which has been produced
from his wounded side and from the depths of his tomb.
All through the services the victory of Christ is
contemplated and the resurrection is proclaimed.

Thomas Hopko

AND let those who are to be baptized be instructed to
wash and cleanse themselves on the fifth day of the
week (Thursday).

Those who are to receive baptism shall fast on the
Preparation (Friday) and on the Sabbath (Saturday). And
on the Sabbath the bishop shall assemble those who are
to be baptized in one place, and shall bid them all to pray
and bow the knee.

And laying his hand on them he shall exorcise every evil
spirit to flee away from them and never to return to them.
And when he has finished exorcizing, let him breathe on
their faces and seal their foreheads and ears and noses
and then let him raise them up.

And they shall spend all the night in vigil, reading the
scriptures to them and instructing them.

The Apostolic Tradition<br>Hippolytus<br>Third century

CHRIST redeemed humankind and gave perfect glory to God principally through his paschal mystery: by dying he destroyed our death and by rising he restored our life. The Easter triduum of the passion and resurrection of Christ is thus the culmination of the entire liturgical year. What Sunday is to the week, the solemnity of Easter is to the liturgical year.

The Easter triduum begins with the evening Mass of the Lord's Supper, reaches its high point in the Easter Vigil, and closes with evening prayer on Easter Sunday.

On Good Friday and, if possible, also on Holy Saturday until the Easter Vigil, the Easter fast is observed everywhere.

The celebration of the Lord's passion takes place on Friday during the afternoon hours.

The Easter Vigil, in the night when Christ rose from the dead, is considered the mother of all vigils. During it the church keeps watch, awaiting the resurrection of Christ and celebrating it in the sacraments. The entire celebration of this vigil should take place at night, beginning after nightfall and ending with dawn.

General Norms for the Liturgical Year

EVEN though we are baptized, what we constantly lose and betray is precisely that which we received at baptism. Therefore Easter is our return every year to our own baptism, whereas Lent is our preparation for that return—the slow and sustained effort to perform, at the end, our own "passage" or "pascha" into the new life in Christ. . . . Each year Lent and Easter are, once again, the rediscovery and the recovery by us of what we were made through our own baptismal death and resurrection.

Alexander Schmemann

THIS is the Pasch:
    holy the feast we celebrate today.
New and holy is the Pasch,
mystic,
all-venerable,
and Christ, who redeemed us,
is the paschal victim.
The Pasch breathes balm,
is great,
was made for the faithful;
the Pasch opens to us
the gates of paradise.
O Pasch, sanctify all believers.                    Early Greek hymn

Introductory rites
Holy Thursday
Roman rite

**W**E should glory in the cross of our Lord
Jesus Christ,
for he is our salvation, our life and our resurrection;
through him we are saved and made free.

**L**ET all mortal flesh keep silence
And stand with fear and trembling,
Pondering nothing earthly minded,
For the King of kings and Lord of lords comes forth
To be sacrificed and given for food to the faithful.
He is preceded by angels' choirs,
By every Principality and Power,
By the many-eyed Cherubim
And the six-winged Seraphim,
Who cover their faces, chanting:
"Alleluia, Alleluia, Alleluia."

Alexander Bogolepov
Hymn from the Liturgy
of St. James
Fifth century

This is not a criminal going to his punishment with the instrument of his own death laid cruelly on his shoulders, but the King of kings and the Lord of lords, making a solemn, royal procession with his cross.

S ING, my tongue, the song of triumph,
Tell the story far and wide;
Tell of dread and final battle,
Sing of Savior crucified;
How upon the cross a victim
Vanquishing in death he died.

He endured the nails, the spitting,
Vinegar and spear and reed;
From that holy body broken
Blood and water forth proceed:
Earth and stars and sky and ocean
By that flood from stain are freed.

Faithful Cross, above all other,
One and only noble tree,
None in foliage, none in blossom,
None in fruit your peer may be;
Sweet the wood and sweet the iron
And your load, most sweet is he.

Bend your boughs, O Tree of glory!
All your rigid branches, bend!
For a while the ancient temper
That your birth bestowed, suspend;
And the king of earth and heaven
Gently on your bosom tend.

Fortunatus
Sixth century

THE Lord said to Moses and Aaron in the land of Egypt, "This month shall stand at the head of your calendar; you shall reckon it the first month of the year. Tell the whole community of Israel: On the tenth of this month every one of your families must procure for itself a lamb, one apiece for each household. If a family is too small for a whole lamb, it shall join the nearest household in procuring one and shall share in the lamb in proportion to the number of persons who partake of it. The lamb must be a year-old male and without blemish. You may take it from either the sheep or the goats. You shall keep it until the fourteenth day of this month, and then, with the whole assembly of Israel present, it shall be slaughtered during the evening twilight. They shall take some of its blood and apply it to the two door posts and the lintel of every house in which they partake of the lamb. That same night they shall eat its roasted flesh with unleavened bread and bitter herbs.

"This is how you are to eat it: with your loins girt, sandals on your feet and your staff in hand, you shall eat like those who are in flight. It is the Passover of the Lord. For on this same night I will go through Egypt, striking down every first-born of the land, both man and beast, and executing judgment on all the gods of Egypt—I, the Lord! But the blood will mark the houses where you are. Seeing the blood, I will pass over you; thus, when I strike the land of Egypt, no destructive blow will come upon you.

Exodus 12:1–8, 11–14
Holy Thursday
Roman rite

"This day shall be a memorial feast for you, which all your generations shall celebrate with pilgrimage to the Lord, as a perpetual institution."

B UT imitate Christ at all times, signing your forehead
with sincerity. This is the sign of his passion, shown
and proven against the devil, if you make it with faith, not
in order to be seen by others, but knowingly setting it
forward as a shield. For, when the adversary sees that its
power comes from the heart, because it shows forth
publicly the image of baptism, he is put to flight. He flies,
not because of your spittle, but because the Spirit within
you blows him away. When Moses made this sign,
rubbing the blood of the slain paschal lamb on the lintels
of the doorposts, he signified the faith which we now have
in the perfect Lamb.

*The Apostolic Tradition*
Hippolytus
Third century

O UR blessing-cup is a communion
with the blood of Christ.

How can I repay the Lord
for his goodness to me?
The cup of salvation I will raise;
I will call on the Lord's name.

O precious in the eyes of the Lord
is the death of his faithful.
Your servant, Lord, your servant am I;
you have loosened my bonds.

My vows to the Lord I will fulfill
before all his people,
in the courts of the house of the Lord,
in your midst, O Jerusalem.

From Psalm 116

I received from the Lord what I handed on to you, namely, that the Lord Jesus on the night in which he was betrayed took bread, and after he had given thanks, broke it and said, "This is my body, which is for you. Do this in remembrance of me." In the same way, after the supper, he took the cup, saying, "This cup is the new covenant in my blood. Do this, whenever you drink it, in remembrance of me."

*1 Corinthians 11:23–26*
*Holy Thursday*
*Roman rite*

Every time, then, you eat this bread and drink this cup, you proclaim the death of the Lord until he comes!

WE proclaim your death, Lord.
We sing to you, O Christ, for your
glorious resurrection.
We have been judged worthy to approach this mystical,
    ineffable banquet.

Let us share, joyfully,
in the spiritual gifts here before us;
let us sing with the angels
the canticle of victory. Alleluia.

The Lord, who abides in the Father's bosom,
is on the cross as well, today;
Of his own will,
he chose to be buried like a mortal man;
but on the third day, he rose again

*Early Christian prayer*    and gave us the gift of his great mercy.

BEFORE the feast of Passover, Jesus realized that the hour had come for him to pass from this world to the Father. He had loved his own in this world, and would show his love for them to the end. The devil had already induced Judas, son of Simon Iscariot, to hand Jesus over; and so, during the supper, Jesus—fully aware that he had come from God and was going to God, the Father who had handed everything over to him—rose from the meal and took off his cloak. He picked up a towel and tied it around himself. Then he poured water into a basin and began to wash his disciples' feet and dry them with the towel he had around him. Thus he came to Simon Peter, who said to him, "Lord, are you going to wash my feet?" Jesus answered, "You may not realize now what I am doing, but later you will understand." Peter replied, "You shall never wash my feet!" "If I do not wash you," Jesus answered, "you will have no share in my heritage." "Lord," Simon Peter said to him, "then not only my feet, but my hands and head as well." Jesus told him, "The man who has bathed has no need to wash [except for his feet]; he is entirely cleansed, just as you are; though not all." (The reason he said, "Not all are washed clean," was that he knew his betrayer.)

After he had washed their feet, he put his cloak back on and reclined at table once more. He said to them:
    "Do you understand what I just did for you?
    You address me as 'Teacher' and 'Lord,'
    and fittingly enough,
    for that is what I am.
    But if I washed your feet—
    I who am Teacher and Lord—
    then you must wash each other's feet.
    What I just did was to give you an example:
    as I have done, so you must do.

John 13:1–15
Holy Thursday
Roman rite

JESUS, come, my feet are dirty. You have become a servant for my sake, so fill your basin with water; come, wash my feet. I know that I am bold in saying this, but your own words have made me fearful: "If I do not wash your feet, you will have no companionship with me." Wash my feet, then, so that I may be your companion. But what am I saying: "Wash my feet"? Peter could say these words, for all that needed washing were his feet. For the rest, he was completely clean. I must be made clean with that other washing of which you said: "I have a baptism with which I must be baptized."

*Origen*
*Third century*

FELLOW servants of our Lord Jesus Christ: On the night before his death, Jesus set an example for his disciples by washing their feet, an act of humble service. He taught that strength and growth in the life of the Kingdom of God come not by power, authority, or even miracle, but by such lowly service. We all need to remember his example, but none stand more in need of this reminder than those whom the Lord has called to the ordained ministry.

Therefore, I invite you who share in the priesthood of Christ, to come forward, that I may recall whose servant I am by following the example of my Master. But come remembering his admonition that what will be done for you is also to be done by you to others, for "a servant is not greater than his master, nor is one who is sent greater than the one who sent him. If you know these things, blessed are you if you do them."

*The Book of*
*Occasional Services*

WHERE charity and love are found,
there is God.

The love of Christ has gathered us together into one.
Let us rejoice and be glad in him.
Let us fear and love the living God,
and love each other from the depths of our heart.

Therefore when we are together,
let us take heed not to be divided in mind.
Let there be an end to bitterness and quarrels,
     an end to strife,
and in our midst be Christ our God.

And, in company with the blessed, may we see
your face in glory, Christ our God,
pure and unbounded joy
for ever and ever.

Procession with gifts
for the poor
Holy Thursday
Roman rite

FATHER, all-powerful and ever-living God,
we do well always and everywhere to give
you thanks.

You decreed that we should be saved through
     the wood of the cross.
The tree of our defeat became our tree of victory;
where life was lost, there life has been restored
through Christ our Lord.

Preface of the Triumph
of the Cross
Roman rite

GOD our Father,
we are gathered here to share in the supper
which your only Son left to his church to reveal
his love.
He gave it to us when he was about to die
and commanded us to celebrate it as the new
and eternal sacrifice.
We pray that in this eucharist
we may find the fullness of love and life.

Opening prayer
Holy Thursday
Roman rite

ALMIGHTY God,
we receive new life
from the supper your Son gave us in this world.
May we find full contentment
in the meal we hope to share
in your eternal kingdom.

Prayer after
communion
Holy Thursday
Roman rite

OF thy mystical supper, O Son of God, accept me
today a communicant, for I will not speak of thy
mystery to thine enemies, neither like Judas will I give
thee a kiss, but like the thief will I confess thee: Remember
me, O Lord, in thy kingdom.

Hymn on
Holy Thursday
Divine Liturgy
of Saint Basil

To know Christ sacramentally only in terms of bread and wine is to know him only partially, in the dining room as host and guest. It is a valid enough knowledge, but its ultimate weakness when isolated is that it is perhaps too civil. . . . However elegant the knowledge of the dining room may be, it begins in the soil, in the barnyard, in the slaughterhouse; amid the quiet violence of the garden, strangled cries, and fat spitting in the pan. Table manners depend on something's having been grabbed by the throat. A knowledge that ignores these dark and murderous human *gestes* is losing its grip on the human condition.

Aidan Kavanagh

THOU who art the Lord of all and God the Creator, thou to whom suffering is unknown, didst humble thyself and unite thyself with thy creation, and as the Passover, thou hast offered thyself to those for whom thou willed to die, saying: "Eat of my body, and be established in faith." Thou didst satisfy thy disciples, O Blessed One, with thine own redeeming cup . . . saying: "Drink of my blood, and be established in faith."

Holy Thursday
Orthodox liturgy

HAIL our Savior's glorious body,
Which his virgin mother bore;
Hail the blood which, shed for sinners,
Did a broken world restore;
Hail the sacrament most holy,
Flesh and blood of Christ adore!

To the virgin, for our healing,
His own Son the Father sends;
From the Father's love proceeding
Sower, seed and word descends;
Wondrous life of word incarnate
With his greatest wonder ends!

On that paschal ev'ning see him
With the chosen twelve recline,
To the Law he is obedient
In its feast of love divine;
Love divine, the new law giving
Gives himself as bread and wine!

Come, adore this wondrous presence;
Bow to Christ, the source of grace!
Here is kept the ancient promise
Of God's earthly dwelling place!
Sight is blind before God's glory,
Faith alone may see his face!

Thomas Aquinas
Thirteenth century

LET the paschal fast be kept sacred. Let it be celebrated everywhere on Good Friday and, where possible, prolonged throughout Holy Saturday, so that the joys of the Sunday of the resurrection may be attained with uplifted and clear mind.

*Constitution on
the Sacred Liturgy*

S EE, my servant shall prosper,
he shall be raised high and greatly exalted.
Even as many were amazed at him—
so marred was his look beyond that of man,
and his appearance beyond that of mortals—
So shall he startle many nations,
because of him kings shall stand speechless;
For those who have not been told shall see,
those who have not heard shall ponder it.

Who would believe what we have heard?
To whom has the arm of the Lord been revealed?
He grew up like a sapling before him,
like a shoot from the parched earth;
There was in him no stately bearing to make us
look at him,
nor appearance that would attract us to him.
He was spurned and avoided by men,
a man of suffering, accustomed to infirmity,
One of those from whom men hide their faces,
spurned, and we held him in no esteem.

Yet it was our infirmities that he bore,
our sufferings that he endured,
While we thought of him as stricken,
as one smitten by God and afflicted.
But he was pierced for our offenses,
crushed for our sins;
Upon him was the chastisement that makes us whole,
by his stripes we were healed.
We had all gone astray like sheep,
each following his own way;
But the Lord laid upon him
the guilt of us all.

Though he was harshly treated, he submitted
and opened not his mouth;

Like a lamb led to the slaughter
    or a sheep before the shearers,
    he was silent and opened not his mouth.
Oppressed and condemned, he was taken away,
    and who would have thought any more of
        his destiny?
When he was cut off from the land of the living,
    and smitten for the sin of his people,
A grave was assigned him among the wicked
    and a burial place with evildoers,
Though he had done no wrong
    nor spoken any falsehood.
[But the Lord was pleased
    to crush him in infirmity.]

If he gives his life as an offering for sin,
    he shall see his descendants in a long life,
    and the will of the Lord shall be accomplished
        through him.

Because of his affliction
    he shall see the light in fullness of days;
Through his suffering, my servant shall justify many,
    and their guilt he shall bear.
Therefore I give him his portion among the great,
    and he shall divide the spoils with the mighty,
Because he surrendered himself to death
    and was counted among the wicked;
Isaiah 52:13–53:12    And he shall take away the sins of many,
Good Friday
Roman rite        and win pardon for their offenses.

IT is immensely easier to suffer in obedience to a human command than to suffer in the freedom of one's own responsible deed. It is immensely easier to suffer with others than to suffer alone. It is immensely easier to suffer openly and honorably than apart and in shame. It is immensely easier to suffer through commitment of the physical life than in the spirit. Christ suffered in freedom, alone, apart and in shame, in body and spirit, and since then many Christians have so suffered with him.  Dietrich Bonhoeffer

LET us exalt our minds, kindle our hearts; let us not quench our spirits,
But let us be uplifted in soul and hasten near by
to suffer with the one incapable of suffering.
Let us lay aside all tiresome arguments
And attach ourselves to the one on the cross.
If it seems right, let us all go along with Peter
To the house of Caiaphas, and with him
Let us cry to Christ the words of Peter long ago—
"Even if he goes to the cross and enters the tomb—
We suffer with you, and we shall die with you
and cry:

'Hasten, Holy One, save your sheep.' "

Romanos
Sixth century

W EARY of all trumpeting,
    Weary of all killing,
Weary of all songs that sing
Promise, nonfulfilling.
We would raise, O Christ, one song:
We would join in singing
That great music pure and strong,
Wherewith heav'n is ringing.

Captain Christ, O lowly Lord,
Servant King, your dying
Bade us sheathe the foolish sword,
Bade us cease denying.
Trumpet with your Spirit's breath
Through each height and hallow:
Into your self-giving death,
Call us all to follow.

To the triumph of your cross
Summon all the living
Summon us to live by loss,
Gaining all by giving.
Suff'ring all, that we may see
Triumph in surrender;
Leaving all, that we may be
Martin Franzmann   Partners in your splendor.

FATHER,
I put my life in your hands.

In you, O Lord, I take refuge.
Let me never be put to shame.
In your justice, set me free.
Into your hands I commend my spirit.
It is you who will redeem me, Lord.

In the face of all my foes
I am a reproach,
an object of scorn to my neighbors
and of fear to my friends.
Those who see me in the street
run far away from me.
I am like a dead man, forgotten,
like a thing thrown away.

But as for me, I trust in you, Lord,
I say: "You are my God.
My life is in your hands, deliver me
from the hands of those who hate me."

Let your face shine on your servant.
Save me in your love.
Be strong, let your heart take courage,
all who hope in the Lord.                    From Psalm 31

WE have a great high priest who has passed through the heavens, Jesus, the Son of God; let us hold fast to our profession of faith. For we do not have a high priest who is unable to sympathize with our weakness, but one who was tempted in every way that we are, yet never sinned. So let us confidently approach the throne of grace to receive mercy and favor and to find help in time of need.

In the days when he was in the flesh, Christ offered prayers and supplications with loud cries and tears to God, who was able to save him from death, and he was heard because of his reverence. Son though he was, he learned obedience from what he suffered; and when perfected, he became the source of eternal salvation for all who obey him.

Hebrews 4:14–16;
5:7–9
Good Friday
Roman rite

YOU love humankind, O Christ, and I glorify you for that. You are the only Son, the Lord of all things. You alone are without sin. You gave yourself up to death for me, an unworthy sinner, the death of the cross. Through this suffering, you have delivered all human beings from the snares of evil. What shall I render to you, Lord, for such goodness?

Glory to you, friend of us all!
Glory to you, O merciful Lord!
Glory to you, longsuffering God!
Glory to you, who takes away all sins!
Glory to you, who came to save us!
Glory to you, who became flesh in the womb
    of the virgin!
Glory to you, bound in cords!
Glory to you, whipped and scourged!
Glory to you, mocked and derided!
Glory to you, nailed to the cross!
Glory to you, buried and risen!
Glory to you, proclaimed to all humankind,
    who believe in you!
Glory to you, ascended to heaven!

Ephraem
Fourth century

S T. JOHN develops aspects of the passion that in some instances are present in rudimentary form in the other gospels but are not spelled out as they are in the fourth gospel. We have in mind especially the voluntary aspect of Christ's death. Jesus hands himself over, and does so with great dignity and on the condition that his disciples are allowed to go free (Jn 18:6–8). Elsewhere, he himself chooses the "hour" when he will surrender to his executioners. . . . In two passages Jesus' use of the word is connected with a theology of his passion and death: "The hour has come for the Son of Man to be glorified" (12:23). But the glorification in no way lessens his burden of anguish: " 'Now is my soul troubled. And what shall I say? "Father, save me from this hour"? No, for this purpose I have come to this hour. Father, glorify thy name.' Then a voice came from heaven, 'I have glorified it, and I will glorify it again' " (12:27–28).

For St. John, then, Christ's cross and death are unintelligible unless they are seen as a sign of his glorification and exaltation. . . . In St. John's gospel, the cross itself is presented as resurrection and glory no less than as death. John certainly depicts the crucifixion as a visible, sensibly real event, but he also insists that it be seen as a sign that contains what it signifies, namely, Christ's glorification. When Christ is dying, he is already going back to the Father (16:17; cf. 14:28; 16:10).

Adrian Nocent

*Most translations of John's gospel, including the New American Bible translation given on the following pages, render* Ioudaioi *as "the Jews." Listening to the reading of the passion from John, one would assume that the author believes the whole Jewish nation was set against Jesus. At the time when this gospel was written, there was a growing antipathy between the Christian and Jewish communities. Is it this historical situation which led the author to speak thus? Some scholars believe that there is another explanation. Gerard Sloyan in the following text explains that* Ioudaioi, *in the passages from the passion, must be understood in context each time it is used and that it would most often be inaccurate to translate* Ioudaioi *as "the Jews."*

I N New Testament times *Ioudaioi* was primarily a geographical denotation (broad or narrow depending on the context) within Palestine. Amongst Gentiles and diaspora Jews it had a secondary religious meaning. For Jews of Palestine, *Israel* was the self-name employed. Non-Judean Jews would be called *Ioudaioi* only because they too had the religion proper to the territory Judea. . . .

Jesus is "King of Israel," i.e., Messiah, in John 1:49 and 12:13 when the connotation is religious but "King of the Judeans" in 18:33 and 19:19, 21 when the charge is political (the latter two the placard giving the charge on which he died). . . . "King of Judea" is the best rendition of the meaning of *basileus ton Ioudaion*. . . .

In nine or ten clear cases *hoi Ioudaioi* means the Sanhedrin and its minions (18:12, 14, 31, 36, 38; 19:7, 12, 14, 31). Just as not all Judeans were against Jesus—enough however, for that fact to be regularly recorded—so only certain ones among the "Judean authorities" were opposed to him. "Judean," not "Jewish" authorities, is probably correct because the Sanhedrin had civil jurisdiction within at most Pilate's sphere (except for Samaria), not elsewhere.

Gerard Sloyan

JESUS went out with his disciples across the Kidron valley. There was a garden there, and he and his disciples entered it. The place was familiar to Judas as well (the one who was to hand him over) because Jesus had often met there with his disciples. Judas took the cohort as well as police supplied by the chief priests and the Pharisees, and came there with lanterns, torches and weapons. Jesus, aware of all that would happen to him, stepped forward and said to them, "Who is it you want?" "Jesus the Nazorean," they replied. "I am he," he answered. (Now Judas, the one who was to hand him over, was right there with them.) As Jesus said to them, "I am he," they retreated slightly and fell to the ground. Jesus put the question to them again, "Who is it you want?" "Jesus the Nazorean," they repeated. "I have told you, I am he," Jesus said. "If I am the one you want, let these men go." (This was to fulfill what he had said, "I have not lost one of those you gave me.")

Then Simon Peter, who had a sword, drew it and struck the slave of the high priest, severing his right ear. (The slave's name was Malchus.) At that Jesus said to Peter, "Put your sword back in its sheath. Am I not to drink the cup the Father has given me?"

Then the soldiers of the cohort, their tribune, and the Jewish police arrested Jesus and bound him. They led him first to Annas, the father-in-law of Caiaphas who was high priest that year. (It was Caiaphas who had proposed to the Jews the advantage of having one man die for the people.)

Simon Peter, in company with another disciple, kept following Jesus closely. This disciple, who was known to the high priest, stayed with Jesus as far as the high priest's courtyard, while Peter was left standing at the gate. The disciple known to the high priest came out and spoke to the woman at the gate, and then brought Peter in. This servant girl who kept the gate said to Peter, "Aren't you one of this man's followers?" "Not I," he replied.

Now the night was cold, and the servants and the guards who were standing around had made a charcoal fire to warm themselves by. Peter joined them and stood there warming himself.

The high priest questioned Jesus, first about his disciples, then about his teaching. Jesus answered by saying:
"I have spoken publicly to any who would listen.
I always taught in a synagogue or in the temple area
    where all the Jews come together.
There was nothing secret about anything I said.
Why do you question me? Question those who heard me when I spoke. It should be obvious they will know what I said." At this reply, one of the guards who was standing nearby gave Jesus a sharp blow on the face. "Is that any way to answer the high priest?" he said. Jesus replied, "If I said anything wrong produce the evidence, but if I spoke the truth why hit me?" Annas next sent him, bound, to the high priest Caiaphas.

All through this, Simon Peter had been standing there warming himself. They said to him, "Are you not a disciple of his?" He denied: "I am not!" "But did I not see you with him in the garden?" insisted one of the high priest's slaves—as it happened, a relative of the man whose ear Peter had severed. Peter denied it again. At that moment a cock began to crow.

At daybreak they brought Jesus from Caiaphas to the praetorium. They did not enter the praetorium themselves, for they had to avoid ritual impurity if they were to eat the Passover supper. Pilate came out to them. "What accusation do you bring against this man?" he demanded. "If he were not a criminal," they retorted, "we would certainly not have handed him over to you." At this Pilate said, "Why do you not take him and pass judgment on him according to your law?" "We may not put anyone to death," the Jews answered. (This was to fulfill what Jesus had said, indicating the sort of death he would die.)

Pilate went back into the praetorium and summoned Jesus. "Are you the King of the Jews?" he asked him. Jesus answered, "Are you saying this on your own, or have others been telling you about me?" "I am no Jew!" Pilate retorted, "It is your own people and the chief priests who have handed you over to me. What have you done?" Jesus answered:

"My kingdom does not belong to this world.
If my kingdom were of this world,
my subjects would be fighting
to save me from being handed over to the Jews.
As it is, my kingdom is not here."

At this Pilate said to him, "So, then, you are a king?" Jesus replied:

"It is you who say I am a king.
The reason I was born,
the reason why I came into the world,
is to testify to the truth.
Anyone committed to the truth hears my voice."

"Truth!" said Pilate, "What does that mean?"

After this remark, Pilate went out again to the Jews and told them: "Speaking for myself, I find no case against this man. Recall your custom whereby I release to you someone at Passover time. Do you want me to release to you the king of the Jews?" "They shouted back, "We want Barabbas, not this one!" (Barabbas was an insurrectionist.)

Pilate's next move was to take Jesus and have him scourged. The soldiers then wove a crown of thorns and fixed it on his head, throwing around his shoulders a cloak of royal purple. Repeatedly they came up to him and said, "All hail, King of the Jews!" slapping his face as they did so.

Pilate went out a second time and said to the crowd: "Observe what I do. I am going to bring him out to you to make you realize that I find no case against him." When Jesus came out wearing the crown of thorns and the purple cloak, Pilate said to them, "Look at the man!" As soon as the chief priests and the temple police saw him they shouted, "Crucify him! Crucify him!" Pilate said,

"Take him and crucify him yourselves; I find no case against him." "We have our law," the Jews responded, "and according to that law he must die because he made himself God's Son." When Pilate heard this kind of talk, he was more afraid than ever.

Going back into the praetorium, he said to Jesus, "Where do you come from?" Jesus would not give him any answer. "Do you refuse to speak to me?" Pilate asked him. "Do you not know that I have the power to release you and the power to crucify you?" Jesus answered:
"You would have no power over me whatever
unless it were given you from above.
That is why he who handed me over to you
is guilty of the greater sin."

After this, Pilate was eager to release him, but the Jews shouted, "If you free this man you are no 'Friend of Caesar.' Anyone who makes himself a king becomes Caesar's rival." Pilate heard what they were saying, then brought Jesus outside and took a seat on a judge's bench at the place called the Stone Pavement—Gabbatha in Hebrew. (It was the Preparation Day for Passover, and the hour was about noon.) He said to the Jews, "Look at your king!" At this they shouted, "Away with him! Away with him! Crucify him!" "What!" Pilate exclaimed. "Shall I crucify your king?" The chief priests replied, "We have no king but Caesar." In the end, Pilate handed Jesus over to be crucified.

Jesus was led away, and carrying the cross by himself, went out to what is called the Place of the Skull (in Hebrew, Golgotha). There they crucified him, and two others with him: one on either side, Jesus in the middle. Pilate had an inscription placed on the cross which read, "Jesus the Nazorean, the King of the Jews." This inscription, in Hebrew, Latin and Greek, was read by many of the Jews, since the place where Jesus was crucified was near the city. The chief priests of the Jews tried to tell Pilate, "You should not have written, 'The

King of the Jews.' Write instead, 'This man claimed to be king of the Jews.' " Pilate answered, "What I have written, I have written."

After the soldiers had crucified Jesus they took his garments and divided them four ways, one for each soldier. There was also his tunic, but this tunic was woven in one piece from top to bottom and had no seam. They said to each other, "We shouldn't tear it. Let's throw dice to see who gets it." (The purpose of this was to have the Scripture fulfilled:

"They divided my garments among them;
for my clothing they cast lots.")

And this is what the soldiers did.

Near the cross of Jesus there stood his mother, his mother's sister, Mary the wife of Clopas, and Mary Magdalene. Seeing his mother there with the disciple whom he loved, Jesus said to his mother, "Woman, there is your son." In turn he said to the disciple, "There is your mother." From that hour onward, the disciple took her into his care.

After that, Jesus, realizing that everything was now finished, to bring the Scripture to fulfillment said, "I am thirsty." There was a jar there, full of common wine. They stuck a sponge soaked in this wine on some hyssop and raised it to his lips. When Jesus took the wine, he said, "Now it is finished." Then he bowed his head, and delivered over his spirit.

Since it was the Preparation Day the Jews did not want to have the bodies left on the cross during the sabbath, for that sabbath was a solemn feast day. They asked Pilate that the legs be broken and the bodies be taken away. Accordingly, the soldiers came and broke the legs of the men crucified with Jesus, first of one, then of the other. When they came to Jesus and saw that he was already dead, they did not break his legs. One of the soldiers ran a lance into his side, and immediately blood and water flowed out. (This testimony has been given by an eyewitness, and his testimony is true. He tells what he

knows is true, so that you may believe.) These events took place for the fulfillment of Scripture:
"Break none of his bones."
There is still another Scripture passage which says:
"They shall look on him whom they have pierced."

Afterward, Joseph of Arimathea, a disciple of Jesus (although a secret one for fear of the Jews), asked Pilate's permission to remove Jesus' body. Pilate granted it, so they came and took the body away. Nicodemus (the man who had first come to Jesus at night) likewise came, bringing a mixture of myrrh and aloes which weighed about a hundred pounds. They took Jesus' body, and in accordance with Jewish burial custom bound it up in wrappings of cloth with perfumed oils. In the place where he had been crucified there was a garden, and in the garden a new tomb in which no one had ever been laid. Because of the Jewish Preparation Day they laid Jesus there, for the tomb was close at hand.

John 18:1–19:42
Good Friday
Roman rite

P ETER, Apostle, have you seen my love so bright?
I saw him with his enemies—a harrowing sight!

Who is that fine man upon the Passion Tree?
It is your Son, dear Mother, know you not me?

Is that the wee babe I bore nine months in my womb
That was born in a stable when no house would give us
     room?

Mother, be quiet, let not your heart be torn,
My keening women, Mother, are yet to be born!

*Refrain*
M'ochon agus m'ochon o!                              An Irish lament

JOSEPH went to Pilate, pleaded with him and cried out:
Give me that Stranger
Who since his youth
Has wandered as a stranger.

Give me that Stranger
Upon whom I look with wonder,
Seeing him a guest of death.

Give me that Stranger
Whom envious men
Estrange from the world.

Give me that Stranger
That I may bury him in a tomb,
Who being a stranger has no place
Whereon to lay his head.

Give me that Stranger
To whom his mother cried out
As she saw him dead:
"My Son, my senses are wounded
And my heart is burned
As I see you dead!
Yet, trusting in your resurrection,
I magnify you!"

In such words did the honorable Joseph plead with Pilate.
He took the Savior's body and, with fear, wrapped it in
linen with spices. And he placed you in a tomb, O you
who grant everlasting life and great mercy to us all.

Holy Saturday
Orthodox liturgy

IN paradise of old the wood stripped me bare. . . .
Now the wood of the cross that clothes us
   with the garment
of life has been set up in the midst of the earth,
And the whole world is filled with boundless joy.

Exaltation of the Cross
Orthodox liturgy

THE general intercessions conclude the liturgy of the word. The priest stands at the chair, or he may be at the lectern or altar. With his hands joined, he sings or says the introduction in which each intention is stated. All kneel and pray silently for some period of time, and then the priest, with hands extended, sings or says the prayer. The people may either kneel or stand throughout the entire period of the general intercessions.

The conference of bishops may provide an acclamation for the people to sing before the priest's prayer or decree that the deacon's traditional invitation to kneel and pray be continued.

In the United States, if desired, an appropriate acclamation by the people may be introduced before each of the solemn prayers of intercession, or the traditional period of kneeling at each of the prayers (at the invitation of the deacon) may be continued.

The priest may choose from the prayers in the missal those which are more appropriate to local circumstances, provided the series follows the rule for the general intercessions.

Good Friday
Roman rite

L ET us pray, dear friends,
for the holy Church of God throughout the world,
that God the almighty Father
guide it and gather it together
so that we may worship him in peace and tranquility.

*Silent prayer*

Almighty and eternal God,
you have shown your glory to all nations
in Christ, your Son.
Guide the work of your Church.
Help it to persevere in faith,
proclaim your name,
and bring your salvation to people everywhere.
We ask this through Christ our Lord.


L ET us pray
for our Holy Father, Pope N.,
that God who chose him to be bishop
may give him health and strength
to guide and govern God's holy people.

*Silent prayer*

Almighty and eternal God,
you guide all things by your word,
you govern all Christian people.
In your love protect the Pope you have chosen for us.
Under his leadership deepen our faith
and make us better Christians.
We ask this through Christ our Lord.

L ET us pray
for N., our bishop,
for all bishops, priests, and deacons;
for all who have a special ministry in the Church
and for all God's people.

*Silent prayer*

Almighty and eternal God
your Spirit guides the Church
and makes it holy.
Listen to our prayers
and help each of us
in his[1] own vocation
to do your work more faithfully.[2]
We ask this through Christ our Lord.


L ET us pray
for those [among us] preparing for baptism,
that God in his mercy
make them responsive to his love,
forgive their sins through the waters of new birth,
and give them life in Jesus Christ our Lord.

*Silent prayer*

Almighty and eternal God,
you continually bless your Church with new members.
Increase the faith and understanding
of those [among us] preparing for baptism.
Give them a new birth in these living waters
and make them members of your chosen family.[3]
We ask this through Christ our Lord.

---

1. Where the official English translation of prayers from the Roman rite is presented, in this book, exclusive language has not been altered.

2. These footnotes give the instances where the *Lutheran Book of Worship* has alternate wording. Here, for "Listen . . . faithfully," LBW has: "Help each of us to do faithfully the work to which you have called us."

3. For "and make . . . family," LBW has "and keep them in the faith and communion of your holy church."

L ET us pray
for all our brothers and sisters
who share our faith in Jesus Christ,
that God may gather and keep together in one Church
all those who seek the truth with sincerity.[4]

*Silent prayer*

Almighty and eternal God,
you keep together those you have united.
Look kindly on all who follow Jesus your Son.
We are all consecrated to you by our common baptism.
Make us one in the fullness of faith,
and keep us one in the fellowship of love.
We ask this through Christ our Lord.

L ET us pray
for the Jewish people,
the first to hear the word of God,
that they may continue to grow in the love of his name
and in faithfulness to his covenant.

*Silent prayer*

Almighty and eternal God,
long ago you gave your promise to Abraham and his
        posterity.
Listen to your Church as we pray
that the people you first made your own
may arrive at the fullness of redemption.
We ask this through Christ our Lord.

---

4. For "who seek the truth with sincerity," LBW has "who know Jesus as
Lord."

L ET us pray
  for those who do not believe in Christ,
that the light of the Holy Spirit
may show them the way to salvation.

*Silent prayer*

Almighty and eternal God,
enable those who do not acknowledge Christ
to find the truth
as they walk before you in sincerity of heart.
Help us to grow in love for one another,
to grasp more fully the mystery of your godhead,
and to become more perfect witnesses of your love
in the sight of men.[5]
We ask this through Christ our Lord.


L ET us pray
  for those who do not believe in God,
that they may find him
by sincerely following all that is right.

*Silent prayer*

Almighty and eternal God,
you created mankind[6]
so that all might long to find you
and have peace when you are found.
Grant that, in spite of the hurtful things
that stand in their way,
they may all recognize in the lives of Christians
the tokens of your love and mercy,
and gladly acknowledge you
as the one true God and Father of us all.
We ask this through Christ our Lord.

---

5. For "men," "all people."
6. For "mankind," "humanity."

L ET us pray
for those who serve us in public office,
that God may guide their minds and hearts,
so that all men may live in true peace and freedom.

*Silent prayer*

Almighty and eternal God,
you know the longings of men's hearts
and you protect their rights.[7]
In your goodness
watch over those in authority,
so that people everywhere may enjoy
religious freedom, security, and peace.[8]
We ask this through Christ our Lord.

L ET us pray, dear friends,
that God the almighty Father
may heal the sick,
comfort the dying,
give safety to travelers,
free those unjustly deprived of liberty,
and rid the world of falsehood,
hunger, and disease.

*Silent prayer*

Almighty, ever-living God,
you give strength to the weary
and new courage to those who have lost heart.
Hear the prayers of all who call on you in any trouble
that they may have the joy of receiving your help in
their need.
Good Friday
Roman rite    We ask this through Christ our Lord.

---

7. For "you know . . . rights," LBW has, "you are the champion of the poor and oppressed."

8. For "religious freedom, security, and peace," LBW has "justice, peace, freedom, and a share in the goodness of your creation."

DEAR People of God: Our heavenly Father sent his Son into the world, not to condemn the world, but that the world through him might be saved; that all who believe in him might be delivered from the power of sin and death, and become heirs with him of everlasting life.

We pray, therefore, for people everywhere according to their needs.

*In the biddings which follow, the indented petitions may be adapted by addition or omission, as appropriate, at the discretion of the Celebrant. The people may be directed to stand or kneel.*

LET us pray for the holy Catholic Church of Christ throughout the world;

> For its unity in witness and service
>
> For all bishops and other ministers and the people whom they serve
>
> For N., our Bishop, and all the people of this diocese
>
> For all Christians in this community
>
> For those about to the baptized (particularly _____)

That God will confirm his Church in faith, increase it in love, and preserve it in peace.

*Silence*

Almighty and everlasting God, by whose Spirit the whole body of your faithful people is governed and sanctified: Receive our supplications and prayers which we offer before you for all members of your holy Church, that in their vocation and ministry they may truly and devoutly serve you; through our Lord and Savior Jesus Christ. Amen.

L ET us pray for all nations and peoples of the earth, and for those in authority among them;

> For N., the President of the United States
>
> For the Congress and the Supreme Court
>
> For the Members and Representatives
>  of the United Nations
>
> For all who serve the common good

That by God's help they may seek justice and truth, and live in peace and concord.

*Silence*

Almighty God, kindle, we pray, in every heart the true love of peace, and guide with your wisdom those who take counsel for the nations of the earth; that in tranquility your dominion may increase, until the earth is filled with the knowledge of your love; through Jesus Christ our Lord.
Amen.

L ET us pray for all who suffer and are afflicted in body or in mind;

> For the hungry and the homeless, the destitute
>  and the oppressed
>
> For the sick, the wounded, and the crippled
>
> For those in loneliness, fear, and anguish
>
> For those who face temptation, doubt,
>  and despair
>
> For the sorrowful and bereaved
>
> For prisoners and captives, and those
>  in mortal danger

That God in his mercy will comfort and relieve them, and grant them the knowledge of his love, and stir up in us the will and patience to minister to their needs.

*Silence*

Gracious God, the comfort of all who sorrow, the strength of all who suffer: Let the cry of those in misery and need come to you, that they may find your mercy present with them in all their afflictions; and give us, we pray, the strength to serve them for the sake of him who suffered for us, your Son Jesus Christ our Lord.
Amen.

L ET us pray for all who have not received the Gospel of Christ;

> For those who have never heard the word
> of salvation

> For those who have lost their faith

> For those hardened by sin or indifference

> For the contemptuous and the scornful

> For those who are enemies of the cross of Christ
> and persecutors of his disciples

> For those who in the name of Christ
> have persecuted others

That God will open their hearts to the truth, and lead them to faith and obedience.

*Silence*

Merciful God, Creator of all the peoples of the earth and lover of souls: Have compassion on all who do not know you as you are revealed in your Son Jesus Christ; let your Gospel be preached with grace and power to those who have not heard it; turn the hearts of those who resist it; and bring home to your fold those who have gone astray; that there may be one flock under one shepherd, Jesus Christ our Lord.
Amen.

L ET us commit ourselves to our God, and pray for the grace of a holy life, that, with all who have departed this world and have died in the peace of Christ, and those whose faith is known to God alone, we may be accounted worthy to enter into the fullness of the joy of our Lord, and receive the crown of life in the day of resurrection.

*Silence*

O God of unchangeable power and eternal light: Look favorably on your whole Church, that wonderful and sacred mystery; by the effectual working of your providence, carry out in tranquility the plan of salvation; let the whole world see and know that things which were cast down are being raised up, and things which had grown old are being made new, and that all things are being brought to their perfection by him through whom all things were made, your Son Jesus Christ our Lord; who lives and reigns with you, in the unity of the Holy Spirit, one God, for ever and ever. Amen.

Good Friday
*Book of*
*Common Prayer*

*Presider:*

B ROTHERS and sisters,
let us lift up our prayers
in the same spirit we lift up the cross:
proclaiming our Lord as
the way that is no dead end,
the truth that cannot be silenced,
and the life that will not be entombed.

*Speaker A:*
FOR the people of our church
   as we strive to fulfill
our many ministries,
let us pray.

*Speaker B:*
For all believers
as we explore
our diverse perspectives,
let us pray.

*Cantor:*
For everyone seeking truth
and searching for community,
let us beg fulfillment
of these deepest needs as
we pray to the Lord:

*All:*
Father, we put our lives in your hands.

*Presider:*
Gracious and loving God,
we have heard your crucified Son
give his dearest ones to one another
and we believe that he gives us to one another
in much the same way.
Pour out your kindness
on this dispersed and often divided family
that calls itself your church,
harmonize our efforts
and gather us together into
the joy and peace of your house.
Amen.

*Speaker C:*

FOR our catechumens
who await the death
and rebirth of baptism,
let us pray.

*Speaker D:*
For all of us
as we reaffirm our ongoing commitment
to the new life within us,
let us pray.

*Cantor:*
For each of us as we approach
thresholds of death and life,
let us live in confidence as
we pray to the Lord:

*All:*
Father, we put our lives in your hands.

*Presider:*
Dying and rising Lord,
because you immersed yourself
in our history
we need not drown
in the turbulence of time;
because you nailed
God's glory to death's tree
our lives, too,
can flower into eternity.
Pass us over into
that fullness of life
which is always your kingdom.
Amen.

*Speaker A:*

FOR our earth
with its lavish but limited resources
and its enthralling but fragile beauty,
let us pray.

*Speaker B:*

For all who lead nations,
who hold powers of destruction
or apply pressures of opinion,
let us pray.

*Speaker C:*

For those who develop
and disburse our world's resources,
let us pray.

*Speaker D:*

For those who shape society's laws
and mold our lifestyles,
let us pray.

*Cantor:*

For every possibility and potential
we have received
let us give thanks as
we pray to the Lord:

*All:*

Father, we put our lives in your hands.

*Presider:*

Creating and sustaining God,
you unfold your power in a universe
which both delights and terrifies us
and which in its immensity
and its intricacy reveals
the vast scope of your concern.
Give us the wisdom
not to despoil this garden greedily
like the children of Adam,
but to tend it carefully
as sons and daughters of God.
Amen.

*Speaker C:*
For ourselves when, like Pilate,
we turn away from truth
and accommodate injustice,
let us pray.

*Speaker D:*
For ourselves when, with Peter,
we defensively deny
what we cherish most dearly,
let us pray.

*Speaker A:*
For ourselves when, like the centurion,
we stab at dead certainty
and find lively mystery,
let us pray.

*Cantor:*
For our every form of rejection
and unbelief
let us ask pardon as
we pray to the Lord:

*All:*
Father, we put our lives in your hands.

*Presider:*
Merciful and compassionate Father,
we know that you have dispatched armies of prophets
to reclaim our faithfulness.
Carry us past the confusing crossfire
of denial and dogma
and enable us to love
freely and fearlessly.
Amen.

*Speaker B:*

FOR men and women
handcuffed by unemployment,
let us pray.

*Speaker C:*

For children
scourged by poverty and prejudice,
let us pray.

*Speaker D:*

For the elderly
whose lives are crowned
with thorns of indifference
and disrespect,
let us pray.

*Speaker A:*

For all who will die uncomforted
or pass from our company unremembered,
let us pray.

*Cantor:*

For our every human sorrow and lack
we ask liberation as we unburden ourselves
and pray to the Lord:

*Presider:*

All-seeing and ever-present God,
no person slips through cracks in your perception
and no event is slurred
in the impeccable precision of your eternity.
Make us all count to one another
as seriously as we do to you;
let not one of us given into your Son's care be lost,
but bring us all to a share in his glory.
Amen.                                            Linda Murphy

L ORD,
by shedding his blood for us,
your Son, Jesus Christ,
established the paschal mystery.
In your goodness, make us holy
and watch over us always.

L ORD,
by the suffering of Christ your Son
you have saved us all from the death
we inherited from sinful Adam.
By the law of nature
we have borne the likeness of his humanity.
May the sanctifying power of grace
help us to put on the likeness of our Lord in heaven,
who lives and reigns for ever and ever.

Opening prayers
Roman rite

ALMIGHTY and eternal God,
you have restored us to life
by the triumphant death and resurrection of Christ.
Continue this healing work within us.
May we who participate in this mystery
never cease to serve you.

Concluding prayer
Roman rite

LORD,
send down your abundant blessing
upon your people who have devoutly recalled the
    death of your son
in the sure hope of the resurrection.
Grant them pardon; bring them comfort.
May their faith grow stronger
and their eternal salvation be assured.

Prayer over the people
Good Friday
Roman rite

*Deacon:*

I am the Savior of all people," says the Lord. "Whatever their troubles, I will answer their cry, and I will always be their God."

*Presider:*
God our Father, we are the work of your hands.

*All:*
Be merciful to your people, Lord.

*Presider:*
You have made yourself known to us through Jesus your Son. *Be merciful . . .*

You breathed your spirit into us, gave us new life. *Be merciful . . .*

Now we are your children, heirs of your kingdom. *Be merciful . . .*

Help us to be holy, to be one in faith and love, to be the sign of your presence in the world. *Be merciful . . .*

*Deacon:*

I am the Savior of all people," says the Lord. "Whatever their troubles, I will answer their cry, and I will always be their God."

*Presider:*
God our Father, you sent Jesus, your Son, to be the light of the world.

*All:*
Be merciful to your people, Lord.

*Presider:*
You sent him to reveal your great love to all nations. *Be merciful . . .*

To set us free from the power of darkness. *Be merciful . . .*

To teach us to worship in spirit and truth. *Be merciful . . .*

But your word has been both heard and unheard, accepted and rejected. *Be merciful . . .*

Extend your kingdom to embrace the world. *Be merciful . . .*

*Deacon:*

I am the Savior of all people," says the Lord. "Whatever their troubles, I will answer their cry, and I will always be their God."

*Presider:*
God our Father, you fashioned the heavens and the earth, all living creatures, wild and tame.

*All:*
Be merciful to your people, Lord.

*Presider:*
All power, all gifts come from you.

You made us stewards of creation to enjoy the fruits of the earth. *Be merciful . . .*

But we have ravaged the land, spoiled what was good, spilled human blood. *Be merciful . . .*

Enlighten our leaders that they may govern with wisdom and justice, seeking peace at all times. *Be merciful . . .*

*Deacon:*

I am the Savior of all people," says the Lord. "Whatever their troubles, I will answer their cry, and I will always be their God."

*Presider:*
God our Father, wherever anyone suffers, there Jesus, your Son, suffers, too.

*All:*
Be merciful to your people, Lord.

*Presider:*
He died that we might understand your love. *Be merciful . . .*

You are our strength in misfortune, our health in weakness, our comfort in sorrow. *Be merciful . . .*

Have pity on us and on all those who yearn for better days. *Be merciful . . .*

*Deacon:*

I am the Savior of all people," says the Lord. "Whatever their troubles, I will answer their cry, and I will always be their God."

Elizabeth-Anne Vanek

B ECAUSE for our sake you tasted gall, may the Enemy's
bitterness be killed in us.

Because for our sake you drank sour wine, may what is
weak in us be strengthened.

Because for our sake you were spat upon, may we be
bathed in the dew of immortality.

Because for our sake you were struck with a rod, may
we receive shelter in the last.

Because for our sake you accepted a crown of thorns,
may we that love you be crowned with garlands
that never can fade.

Because for our sake you were wrapped in a shroud,
may we be clothed in your all-enfolding strength.

Because you were laid in the new grave and the tomb,
may we receive renewal of soul and body.

Because you rose and returned to life, may we be
brought to life again.

Communion hymn
Fifth century

THIS is the wood of the cross, on which hung
the Savior of the world.
Come, let us worship.

Good Friday
Roman rite

WE worship you, Lord,
we venerate your cross,
we praise your resurrection.
Through the cross you brought joy to the world.

May God be gracious and bless us;
and let his face shed its light upon us.

Good Friday
Roman rite

HOW splendid the cross of Christ! It brings life, not
death; light, not darkness; Paradise, not its loss. It is
the wood on which the Lord, like a great warrior, was
wounded in hands and feet and side, but healed thereby
our wounds. A tree had destroyed us, a tree now brought
us life.

Theodore of Studios
Ninth century

THE head that once was crowned with thorns
Is crowned with glory now;
A royal diadem adorns
The mighty victor's brow.

The highest place that heav'n affords
Is his by sov'reign right,
The King of kings, the Lord of lords,
All heaven's eternal light.

The joy of all who dwell above,
The joy of all below
To whom he manifests his love,
And grants his name to know;

To them the cross, with all its shame,
With all its grace, is given;
Their name, an everlasting name,
Their joy, the joy of heaven.

They suffer with their Lord below;
They reign with him above;
Their profit and their joy to know
The mystery of his love.

The cross he bore is life and health,
Though shame and death to him;
His people's hope, his people's wealth,
Their everlasting theme!

Thomas Kelly
Nineteenth century

THE royal banners forward go,
The cross shines forth in mystic glow
Where he, by whom our flesh was made,
In that same flesh our ransom paid.

Where deep for us the spear was dyed,
Life's torrent rushing from his side,
To wash us in the precious flood
Where flowed the water and the blood.

Fulfilled is all that David told
In true prophetic song of old,
That God the nation's king should be
And reign in triumph from the tree.

O tree of beauty, tree most fair,
Ordained those holy limbs to bear:
Gone is your shame, each crimsoned bough
Proclaims the King of glory now.

Blest tree, whose chosen branches bore
The wealth that did the world restore,
The price of humankind to pay
And spoil the spoiler of his prey.

O cross, our one reliance, hail!
Still may your pow'r with us avail
More good for righteous souls to win;
And save the sinner from the sin.

Fortunatus
Sixth century

HOLY is God!
Holy and strong!
Holy immortal One,
have mercy on us!

Ancient acclamation
Veneration
of the Cross
Roman rite

REJOICE, O life-bearing Cross,
The invincible trophy of godliness,
The door of paradise,
The foundation of the faithful,
The protection guarding the church, by which
    corruption is utterly destroyed and the power of
    death swallowed up and we are exalted to heaven
    from earth.
The invincible weapon,
The adversary of demons,
The glory of martyrs,
The true beauty of saints,
The haven of salvation which gives great mercy to
    the world.

Exaltation of the Cross
Orthodox liturgy

REJOICE, O Guide to the blind,
The healer of the sick,
The resurrection of the dead.
O precious Cross which raises us who have fallen
    into corruption,
By which the curse is destroyed and incorruption
    blossoms forth,
By which we earthborn creatures are deified and
    the devil utterly destroyed.
We behold you today exalted in the hands of the
    high priest.
We exalt him who was lifted upon you.
And we venerate you from which we richly draw
    great mercy.

Exaltation of the Cross
Orthodox liturgy

M y God, my God, why have you forsaken me?
You are far from my plea and the cry
of my distress.
O my God, I call by day and you give no reply;
I call by night and I find no peace.

Yet you, O God, are holy,
enthroned on the praises of Israel.
In you our ancestors put their trust;
they trusted and you set them free.
When they cried to you, they escaped.
In you they trusted and never in vain.

But I am a worm and no man,
the butt of men, laughing-stock of the people.
All who see me deride me.
They curl their lips, they toss their heads.
"He trusted in the Lord, let him save him:
let him release him if this is his friend."

Yet, it was you who took me from the womb,
entrusted me to my mother's breast.
To you I was committed from my birth,
from my mother's womb you have been my God.
Do not leave me alone in my distress;
come close, there is none else to help.

Many bulls have surrounded me,
fierce bulls of Bashan close me in.
Against me they open wide their jaws,
like lions, rending and roaring.

Like water I am poured out,
disjointed are all my bones.
My heart has become like wax,
it is melted within my breast.
Parched as burnt clay is my throat,
my tongue cleaves to my jaws.

Many dogs have surrounded me,
a band of the wicked beset me.
They tear holes in my hands and my feet
and lay me in the dust of death.

I can count every one of my bones.
These people stare at me and gloat;
they divide my clothing among them.
They cast lots for my robe.

O Lord, do not leave me alone,
my strength, make haste to help me!
Rescue my soul from the sword,
my life from the grip of these dogs.
Save my life from the jaws of these lions,
my poor soul from the horns of these oxen.

I will tell of your name to my people
and praise you where they are assembled.
"You who fear the Lord give him praise;
all children of Jacob, give him glory.
Revere him, Israel's children.

For he has never despised
nor scorned the poverty of the poor.
From them he has not hidden his face,
but he heard the poor when they cried."

You are my praise in the great assembly.
My vows I will pay before those who fear him.
The poor shall eat and shall have their fill.
They shall praise the Lord, those who seek him.
May their hearts live for ever and ever!

All the earth shall remember and return to the Lord,
all families of the nations worship before him
for the kingdom is the Lord's; he is ruler of the nations.
They shall worship him, all the mighty of the earth;
before him shall bow all who go down to the dust.

And my soul shall live for him, my children serve him.
They shall tell of the Lord to generations yet to come,
declare his faithfulness to people yet unborn:
"These things the Lord has done."

Psalm 22
Office of Readings
Roman rite

How lonely she is now,
the once crowded city!
Widowed is she
who was mistress over nations;
The princess among the provinces
has been made a toiling slave.

Bitterly she weeps at night,
tears upon her cheeks,
With not one to console her
of all her dear ones;
Her friends have all betrayed her
and become her enemies.

Rise up, shrill in the night,
at the beginning of every watch;
Pour out your heart like water
in the presence of the Lord;
Lift up your hands to him
for the lives of your little ones
Who faint from hunger
at the corner of every street.

Lamentations
1:1–2; 2:19

S ING O my love, O my love, my love, my love;
This have I done for my true love.

Tomorrow shall be my dancing day:
  I would my true love did so chance
To see the legend of my play,
  To call my true love to my dance.

For thirty pence Judas me sold,
  His covetousness for to advance;
"Mark whom I kiss, the same do hold,"
  The same is he shall lead the dance.

Then on the cross hanged I was,
  Where a spear to my heart did glance;
There issued forth both water and blood,
  To call my true love to my dance.

Then down to hell I took my way
  For my true love's deliverance,
And rose again on the third day,
  Up to my true love and the dance.                 "My Dancing Day"

B Y the cross which did to death our only Savior,
This blessed vine from which grapes are gathered in:
Jesus Christ, we thank and bless you!
By the cross, which casts down fire upon our planet,
This burning bush in which love is plainly shown:
Jesus Christ, we glorify you!
By the Cross on Calvary's hill securely planted,
This living branch which can heal our every sin:
Conquering God, we your people proclaim you!

By the blood with which we marked the wooden lintels
For our protection the night when God passed by:
Jesus Christ, we thank and bless you!
By the blood, which in our exodus once saved us,
When hell was sealed up by God's engulfing sea:
Jesus Christ, we glorify you!
By the blood which kills the poison in bad fruitage,
And gives new life to the dead sap in the tree:
Conquering God, we your people proclaim you!

By the death on Calvary's hill of him the first-born,
Who bears the wood and the flame of his own pyre:
Jesus Christ, we thank and bless you!
By the death, amid the thorns, of God's own shepherd,
The paschal lamb who was pierced by our despair:
Jesus Christ, we glorify you!
By the death of God's beloved outside his vineyard,
That he might change us from murderer into heir:
Conquering God, we your people proclaim you!

By the wood which sings a song of nuptial gladness,
Of God who takes for his bride our human race:
Jesus Christ, we thank and bless you!
By the wood which raises up in his full vigor
The Son of Man who draws us all by his grace:
Jesus Christ, we glorify you!

By the wood where he perfects his royal priesthood
In one high priest who for sin is sacrifice:
Conquering God, we your people proclaim you!

Holy tree which reaches up from earth to heaven
That all the world may exult in Jacob's God:
Jesus Christ, we thank and bless you!
Mighty ship which snatches us from God's deep anger,
Saves us, with Noah, from drowning in the flood:
Jesus Christ, we glorify you!
Tender wood which gives to brackish water sweetness,
And from the rock shall strike fountains for our good:
Conquering God, we your people proclaim you.                    Didier Rimaud

O Heaven, be struck with horror; earth be plunged
  in chaos;
  Do not dare, Sun, to behold
  Your master on the cross, hanging there of his
    own will,
Let rock be shattered, for the rock of life is now
    wounded by nails. . . .
In fact, let all creation shudder and groan at the passion
    of the Creator.

Adam alone exults.                                              Romanos
                                                               Sixth century

A T the cross her station keeping
Stood the mournful Mother weeping
Close to Jesus at the last.

In the Passion of my Maker
Be my sinful soul partaker,
   May I with her bear my part.

Of his passion bear the token,
In a spirit bowed and broken
   Bear his death within my heart.

May his wounds both wound and heal me,
He enkindle, cleanse, anneal me,
   Be his cross my hope and stay.

*Thirteenth century*

O Death, I will be your death.
  O Grave, I will be your destruction.

*Liturgy of the Hours*
*Roman rite*

O faithful, come, let us behold our Life laid in a tomb to give life to those who dwell in tombs. Come, let us behold him in his sleep and cry out to him with the voice of the prophets: "You are like a lion. Who shall arouse you, O King? Rise by your own power, O you who have given yourself up for us, O Lover of humankind."

The great Moses foretold this day when he said: "God blessed the Seventh Day." For this is the blessed Sabbath, the day of rest on which the only-begotten Son of God abstained from bodily work, as he had ordained that it would occur in death. Through his resurrection, he returned to what had been his state, and in his goodness and love for humankind, bestowed eternal life upon us.

Holy Saturday
Orthodox liturgy

THE elect should be instructed that on Holy Saturday they should rest from their ordinary work as far as possible, spend time in prayer and recollection of mind, and fast according to their ability.

That same day, if there is a meeting of the elect, some of the immediately preparatory rites may be celebrated, such as the recitation of the profession of faith, the ephpheta or opening of ears and mouths, the choosing of a Christian name, and, if it is to be done, the anointing with the oil of catechumens.

*Rite of Christian
Initiation of Adults*

SOMETHING strange is happening—there is a great silence on earth today, a great silence and stillness. The whole earth keeps silence because the King is asleep. The earth trembled and is still because God has fallen asleep in the flesh and he has raised up all who have slept ever since the world began. God has died in the flesh and hell trembles with fear.

He has gone to search for our first parent, as for a lost sheep. Greatly desiring to visit those who live in darkness and in the shadow of death, he has gone to free from sorrow the captives Adam and Eve, he who is both God and the son of Eve. The Lord approached them bearing the cross, the weapon that had won him the victory. At the sight of him Adam, the first man he had created, struck his breast in terror and cried out to everyone: "My Lord be with you all." Christ answered him: "And with your spirit." He took him by the hand and raised him up, saying, "Awake, O sleeper, and rise from the dead, and Christ will give you light."

I am your God, who for your sake have become your son. Out of love for you and for your descendants I now by my own authority command all who are held in bondage to come forth, all who are in darkness to be enlightened, all who are sleeping to arise. I order you, O sleeper, to awake. I did not create you to be held a prisoner in hell. Rise from the dead, for I am the life of the dead. Rise up, work of my hands, you who were created in my image. Rise, let us leave this place, for you are in me and I am in you; together we form only one person and we cannot be separated.

For your sake I, your God, became your son; I, the Lord, took the form of a slave; I, whose home is above the heavens, descended to the earth and beneath the earth. For your sake, for the sake of man, I became like a man without help, free among the dead. For the sake of you, who left a garden, I was betrayed in a garden, and I was crucified in a garden.

See on my face the spittle I received in order to restore to you the life I once breathed into you. See there the marks of the blows I received in order to refashion your warped nature in my image. On my back see the marks of the scourging I endured to remove the burden of sin that weighs upon your back. See my hands, nailed firmly to a tree, for you who once wickedly stretched out your hand to a tree.

I slept on the cross and a sword pierced my side for you who slept in paradise and brought forth Eve from your side. My side has healed the pain in yours. My sleep will rouse you from your sleep in hell. The sword that pierced me has sheathed the sword that was turned against you.

Rise, let us leave this place. The enemy led you out of the earthly paradise. I will not restore you to that paradise, but I will enthrone you in heaven. I forbade you the tree that was only a symbol of life, but see, I who am life itself am now one with you. I appointed cherubim to guard you as slaves are guarded, but now I make them worship you as God. The throne formed by cherubim awaits you, its bearers swift and eager. The bridal chamber is adorned, the banquet is ready, the eternal dwelling places are prepared, the treasure houses of all good things lie open. The kingdom of heaven has been prepared for you from all eternity.

From an ancient homily
Office of Readings
Holy Saturday
Roman rite

TODAY Hades tearfully sighs: "Would that I had not received him who was born of Mary, for he came to me and destroyed my power; he broke my bronze gates, and being God, delivered the souls I had been holding captive." O Lord, glory to your cross and to your holy resurrection!

Today Hades groans: "My power has vanished. I received one who died as mortals die, but I could not hold him: with him and through him, I lost those over which I had ruled. I had held control over the dead since the world began, and lo, he raises them all up with him!" O Lord, glory to your cross and to your holy resurrection.

Holy Saturday
Orthodox liturgy

O Christ, thou didst sleep a life-giving sleep
in the grave,
and didst awaken humankind from the heavy sleep
of sin.

Holy Saturday
Orthodox liturgy

THE Devil speaks:
  Now then, Hades, mourn
 and I join in unison with you in wailing.
Let us lament as we see
  the tree which we planted
Changed into a holy trunk.
Robbers, murderers, tax gatherers, harlots,
Rest beneath it, and make nests
In its branches
  in order that they might gather
The fruit of sweetness
  from the supposedly sterile wood.
For they cling to the cross as the tree of life.

Romanos
Sixth century

O Lord, my God, I sing unto thee a burial song
  and a funeral chant,
who by thy burial hath opened for me a door to life,
and by thy death hath brought an end to death
  and hell.

Holy Saturday
Orthodox liturgy

S ING hymns to him, O earth-born; praise the one
who suffered
And died for you, and when in a short time
You behold him living, receive him in your hearts;
For Christ is going to be resurrected from the tomb
and he will make you new. . . .
Make ready for him a pure heart
In order that your King will dwell in it,
making a heaven.
Only a short time now, and he will come to fill with joy
those who are afflicted,
In order that Adam might exult.

Romanos
Sixth century

A LL-POWERFUL and ever-living God,
your only Son went down among the dead
And rose again in glory.
In your goodness
raise up your faithful people
buried with him in baptism,
to be one with him
in the eternal life of heaven.

Liturgy of the Hours
Roman rite

WE, beloved, will celebrate, as we ought,
Christ's baptism and his holy resurrection,
that gave us life and gave the world salvation:
which may we all achieve through Jesus Christ,
our Lord, and through his grace and kindness.
Glory, worship, honor are his due.

Fourth century

DEAR friends in Christ,
on this most holy night,
when our Lord Jesus Christ passed from death to life,
the church invites her children throughout the world
to come together in vigil and prayer.
This is the passover of the Lord:
if we honor the memory of his death and resurrection
by hearing his word and celebrating his mysteries.
then we may be confident
that we shall share his victory over death
and live with him for ever in God.

Greeting
Roman rite

FATHER,
we share in the light of your glory
through your Son, the light of the world.
Make this new fire holy, and inflame us with new hope.
Purify our minds by this Easter celebration
and bring us one day to the feast of eternal light.

Blessing of fire
Roman rite

NOW, O Lord and God, our Savior Jesus Christ, grant spiritual and physical light to our minds and hearts that had been blinded with worldly errors; enlighten us as you enlightened the holy Marys and the holy women who came to your tomb with spices, so they could sprinkle your holy body, the source of life. . . . Since you have raised us up and delivered us from the stain of our sins and the darkness of our transgressions, make us worthy in your loving kindness to kindle our lamps with today's light, the symbol of your radiant and glorious resurrection.

Wisdom! Let us stand! The light of Christ enlightens all people. Blessed be the Father, the Son and the Holy Spirit who enlighten and sanctify our souls and bodies at all times, now and always and for ever and ever.

*Prayer for the new light Orthodox liturgy*

CHRIST yesterday and today
the beginning and the end
Alpha
and Omega
all time belongs to him
and all the ages
to him be glory and power
through every age for ever.

*Lighting of the candle Roman rite*

BY his holy and glorious wounds
may Christ our Lord guard us and keep us.

*Lighting of the candle Roman rite*

M AY the light of Christ, rising in glory,
dispel the darkness of our hearts and minds.

Lighting of the candle
Roman rite

C OME, O Faithful, and take light from the Light
that never fades;
come and glorify Christ who is risen from the dead!

Christ is risen from the dead!
He has crushed death by his death
and bestowed life upon those who lay in the tomb.

Let God arise and his enemies will scatter
and those who hate him will flee before him.

Easter Sunday
Orthodox liturgy

O night more light than day,
more bright than the sun,
O night more white than snow,
more brilliant than many torches,
O night of more delight than is paradise.

Night devoid of all dark,
O night dispelling sleep
and teaching us the vigilance of angels,
O night the demons tremble at,
night of all nights in all the year desired.

Night of the church's bridal,
night of new birth in baptism,
night when the Devil slept and was stripped,
night when the heir took the heiress
to enjoy their inheritance.

Asterius of Amasia
Fourth century

THIS is the paschal feast, the Lord's passing:
so cried the Spirit.
No type or telling, this,
no shadow;
Pasch of the Lord it is, and truly.
The blood that is shed is a sign of the blood to be shed,
the first indication of what the Spirit will be,
a glimpse of the great anointing.
"I, seeing the blood, will protect you."

You have indeed protected us, Jesus,
from endless disaster.
You spread your hands like a Father
and fatherlike gave cover with your wings.
Your blood, a God's blood, you poured over the earth,
sealing a blood-bargain
for us because you loved us.
What anger threatened you turned away from us;
instead you gave us back God's friendship.

The heavens may have your spirit, paradise your soul
but O may the earth have your blood.

This feast of the Spirit
leads the mystic dance through the year.
The pasch came from God, came from heaven to earth:
from earth it has gone back to heaven.
New is this feast and all-embracing;
all creation assembles at it.

Joy to all creatures, honor, feasting, delight.
Dark death is destroyed
and life is restored everywhere.
The gates of heaven are open.
God has shown himself human,
humanity has gone up to him a God.
The gates of hell God has shattered,
the bars of Adam's prison broken.

The people of the world below have risen
   from the dead,
bringing good news:
what was promised is fulfilled.
From the earth has come singing and dancing.

This is God's passing.
Heaven's God, showing no meanness,
has joined us to himself in the Spirit.
The great marriage-hall is full of guests,
all dressed for the wedding, no guest rejected
for want of a wedding-dress.
The paschal light is the bright new lamp-light,
light that shines from the virgins' lamps.
The light in the soul will never go out.
The fire of grace burns in us all,
spirit, divine,
in our bodies and in our souls,
fed with the oil of Christ.

We pray you, God, our Sovereign, Christ,
King for ever in the world of spirits,
stretch out your strong hands over your holy church
and over the people that will always be yours.
Defend, protect, preserve them,
fight and do battle for them,
subject their enemies to them,
subdue the invisible powers that oppose them,
as you have already subdued those that hate us.
Raise now the sign of victory over us
and grant that we may sing with Moses the song
   of triumph.
For yours are victory and power
for ever and ever. Amen.

Attributed to
Hippolytus
Third century

REJOICE, heavenly powers! Sing, choirs of angels!
Exult, all creation around God's throne!
Jesus Christ, our King, is risen!
Sound the trumpet of salvation!

Rejoice, O earth, in shining splendor,
   radiant in the brightness of your King!
   Christ has conquered! Glory fills you!
   Darkness vanishes for ever!

Rejoice, O Mother Church! Exult in glory!
   The risen Savior shines upon you!
   Let this place resound with joy,
   echoing the mighty song of all God's people!

My dearest friends, standing with me in this holy light,
   join me in asking God for mercy,
   that he may give his unworthy minister
   grace to sing his Easter praises.

Lift up your hearts.
We lift them up to the Lord.
Let us give thanks to the Lord our God.
It is right to give him thanks and praise.

It is truly right
   that with full hearts and minds and voices
   we should praise the unseen God,
      the all-powerful Father,
   and his only Son, our Lord Jesus Christ.

For Christ has ransomed us with his blood,
   and paid for us the price of Adam's sin
   to our eternal Father!

This is our passover feast,
   when Christ, the true Lamb, is slain,
      whose blood consecrates the homes of all believers.

This is the night when first you saved our ancestors:
  you freed the people of Israel from their slavery
  and led them dry-shod through the sea.

This is the night when the pillar of fire
  destroyed the darkness of sin!

This is the night when Christians everywhere,
  washed clean of sin
  and freed from all defilement
  are restored to grace and grow together in holiness.

This is the night when Jesus Christ
  broke the chains of death
  and rose triumphant from the grave.

What good would life have been to us,
  had Christ not come as our Redeemer?

Father, how wonderful your care for us!
  How boundless your merciful love!
  To ransom a slave
  you gave away your Son.

O happy fault, O necessary sin of Adam,
  which gained for us so great a Redeemer!

Most blessed of all nights, chosen by God
  to see Christ rising from the dead!

Of this night scripture says:
  "The night will be as clear as day:
  it will become my light, my joy."

The power of this holy night
  dispels all evil, washes guilt away,
  restores lost innocence, brings mourners joy;
  it casts out hatred, brings us peace,
    and humbles earthly pride.

Night truly blessed when heaven is wedded to earth
and we are reconciled with God.

Therefore, heavenly Father, in the joy of this night,
receive our evening sacrifice of praise,
your Church's solemn offering.

Accept this Easter candle,
a flame divided but undimmed,
a pillar of fire that glows to the honor of God.

Let it mingle with the lights of heaven
and continue bravely burning
to dispel the darkness of this night!

May the Morning Star which never sets
find this flame still burning:
Christ, that Morning Star, who came back
from the dead,
and shed his peaceful light on all humankind,
your Son who lives and reigns for ever and ever.

Exsultet
Roman rite

To those who are not of the household of faith, what we are about to do must look very peculiar. We are about to stand in the dark, carry candles about, sing lengthy and sublime religious texts, read stories from the Bible. What does this all mean? What is going on here in this community?

I think that I first came to understand what this was all about and why I came to think that this was the most important thing in my life when I read *The Lord of the Rings* by J. R. R. Tolkien. In their wandering and meandering, two of the main characters, called hobbits, meet a talking tree, called an Ent, and they introduce themselves and the conversation proceeds:

"I'm a Brandybuck, Meriadoc Brandybuck, though most people call me just Merry."

"And I'm a Took, Peregin Took, but I'm generally called Pippin, or even Pip."

"Hm, but you *are* hasty folk, I see," said Treebeard. "I am honored by your confidence; but you should not be too free all at once. There are Ents and Ents, you know; or there are Ents and things that look like Ents but ain't, as you might say. I'll call you Merry and Pippin, if you please—nice names. For I am not going to tell you *my* name, not yet at any rate." A queer half-knowing, half-humorous look came with a green flicker into his eyes. "For one thing it would take a very long while: my name is growing all the time, and I've lived a very long, long time; so *my* name is like a story. Real names tell you the story of the things they belong to in my language, in the Old Entish as you might say. It is a lovely language, but it takes a very long time to say anything in it, because we do not say anything in it, unless it is worth taking a long time to say, and to listen to."

To use Treebeard's mode of expression, we are not going to be hasty folk tonight, satisfied with glibly saying the name "Christian." Tonight, you might say, is "Old Entish" night in the church. Tonight we are going to tell our name—to ourselves, by way of reminder, to those who will become part of us this night through baptism and confirmation, and to those of the world who will listen, who will take the time to hear what our name is.

And our name is a very long one, one that has been growing since the creation of the world. Our name is a very long story—of how we were made, of how God chose us from among all peoples, of how God liberated us from bondage, of how God planted us in the promised land, of how, in these last times, God has given the story a new twist, given our name meaning in the life, death and resurrection of Jesus.

Because we have been here for so long, it takes a long time to tell who we are, to recount the story of our life as a people. And none of us would be here if we did not think that that name was worth telling and listening to. Now the trick to this kind of name telling is to relax. You cannot be hasty in this time ahead of us. Haste will stop up your ears finally, and then you will not hear this lovely language and our beautiful name.

Relax and make yourself comfortable in the darkness and don't even try to "make sense" of the name. Just hear it, let it roll over you in waves of meanings. Tonight we are going to listen to a series of episodes, not write a theological treatise on the resurrection. A practical word about relaxing: if you need to get up and move about, do so. If you need a breath of fresh air, go out to get it. We'll still be telling the story when you rejoin us. Whatever you need to do to stay comfortable, do it. All of this will enable you to hear the lovely language in which we can really name ourselves as God himself has named us.

Brian Helge    "Christian" is merely an inadequate abbreviation for what we are about to tell.

W E read in the sacramentary that "it must always be borne in mind that the reading of the word of God is the fundamental element of the Easter Vigil." The celebration of the sacraments of initiation may be the center of the night's liturgy, but the scripture reading is the foundation. The structure of this service has each reading followed by a collect, very often with a psalm or canticle and period of silence between the two. The list of readings has varied from one tradition to another, from one century to another, but certain texts occur again and again: the creation, Abraham and Isaac, the exodus, Jonah, passages from Isaiah, the vision of the dry bones, the story of the three young men from Daniel. The lists found in the present liturgical books reflect the various strands of our tradition. In the chart that follows, the scriptures are listed in the order in which they are read. Psalms and canticles are given in parentheses.

| **Roman** (Middle Ages to 1965) | **Roman** (Gregorian) | **Roman** (Current) |
|---|---|---|
| Gn 1:1–2:2<br>*The days of creation* | Gn 1:1–2:2 | Gn 1:1–2:2 (Psalm 104:1–2, 5–6, 10, 12–14, 24, 35 or Psalm 33:4–7, 12–13, 20, 22) |
| Gn 5:32–6:22; 7:6, 11–14, 18–24; 8:1–3, 6–12, 15–21<br>*Noah and the flood* | | |
| Gn 22:1–19<br>*Abraham and Isaac* | | Gn 22:1–18<br>(Psalm 16:5, 8–11) |
| Ex 14:24–15:1<br>*Crossing the Red Sea* | Ex 14:24–15:1<br>(Ex 15:1–2) | Ex 14:15–15:1<br>(Ex 15:1–6, 17–18) |
| *The tender and eternal love of the Lord* | | Is 54:5–14<br>(Psalm 30:1, 3–5, 10–12) |
| Is 54:17–55:11<br>*The everlasting covenant* | | Is 55:1–11<br>(Is 12:2–6) |
| Bar 3:9–38<br>*Praise of wisdom* | | Bar 3:9–15, 32; 4:1–4<br>(Psalm 19:7–10) |
| *Sprinkling of clean water* | | Ez 36:16–28 (Psalm 42:2, 4; 43:3, 4 or Is 12:2–6 or Psalm 51:10–13, 16–17) |
| Ez 37:1–14<br>*Vision of the dry bones* | | |
| Is 4:1–6 (Is 5:1–2)<br>*The Lord's glory, our shelter and shade* | Is 4:2–6<br>(Is 5:1–2) | |
| Ex 12:1–11<br>*The Passover ritual* | | |
| Jon 3:1–10<br>*Repentance of Nineveh* | | |
| Dt 31:22–30<br>(Dt 32:1–4)<br>*The song of Moses* | Dt 31:22–30<br>(Dt 32:1–4) | |
| Dn 3:1–24<br>*The three young men in the fiery furnace* | | |
| *The Lord gathering the remnant* | | |

| Lutheran Book of Worship | Book of Common Prayer | Byzantine tradition |
|---|---|---|
| Gn 1:1–2:2 *or* 1:1–3:24 | Gn 1:1–2:2 (Psalm 33:1–11 *or* Psalm 36:5–10) | Gn 1:1–14 |
| Gn 7:1–5, 11–18; 8:6–18; 9:8–13 | Gn 7:1–5, 11–18; 8:6–18; 9:8–13 (Psalm 46) | |
| Gn 22:1–18 | Gn 22:1–18 (Psalm 33:12–22 *or* Psalm 16) | |
| Ex 14:10–15:1 *or* 13:17–15:1 (Ex 15:1–2, 6, 11, 13, 17) | Ex 14:10–15:1 (Ex 15:1–6, 11–13, 17–18) | Ex 13:20–15:19 |
| Is 55:1–11 | Is 55:1–11 (Is 12:2–6 *or* Psalm 42:1–7) | |
| Bar 3:9–37 | | |
| | Ez 36:24–28 (Psalm 42:1–7 *or* Is 12:2–6) | |
| Ez 37:1–14 | Ez 37:1–14 (Psalm 30 *or* Psalm 143) | Ez 37:1–14 |
| Is 4:2–6 (Is 5:1–2, 7) | Is 4:2–6* (Psalm 122) | |
| Ex 12:1–14 *or* 12:1–24 | | Ex 12:1–11 |
| Jon 3:1–10 | | Jon (entire) |
| Dt 31:19–30 (Dt 32:1–4, 7, 36, 43) | | |
| Dn 3:1–29 (Dn 3:57–87) | | Dn 3:1–56 |
| | Zep 3:12–20 (Psalm 98 *or* Psalm 126) | Zep 3:8–15† |

\* This reading precedes Isaiah 55.

† The Byzantine tradition also includes the following: Is 60:1–16; Jos 5:10–15; 1 Kgs 17:8–24; Is 61:10–62:5; Gn 22:1–18; Is 61:1–9; 2 Kgs 4:8–37; Is 63:11–64:5; Jer 31:31–34.

IN the beginning, when God created the heavens and the earth, the earth was formless wasteland, and darkness covered the abyss, while a mighty wind swept over the waters.

Then God said, "Let there be light," and there was light. God saw how good the light was. God then separated the light from the darkness. God called the light "day," and the darkness he called "night." Thus evening came, and morning followed—the first day.

Then God said, "Let there be a dome in the middle of the waters, to separate one body of water from the other." And so it happened: God made the dome, and it separated the water above the dome from the water below it. God called the dome "the sky." Evening came, and morning followed—the second day.

Then God said, "Let the water under the sky be gathered into a single basin, so that the dry land may appear." And so it happened: the water under the sky was gathered into its basin, and the dry land appeared. God called the dry land "the earth," and the basin of the water he called "the sea." God saw how good it was. Then God said, "Let the earth bring forth vegetation: every kind of plant that bears seed and every kind of fruit tree on earth that bears fruit with its seed in it." And so it happened: the earth brought forth every kind of plant that bears seed and every kind of fruit tree on earth that bears fruit with its seed in it. God saw how good it was. Evening came, and morning followed—the third day.

Then God said: "Let there be lights in the dome of the sky, to separate day from night. Let them mark the fixed time, the days and the years, and serve as luminaries in the dome of the sky, to shed light upon the earth." And so it happened: God made the two great lights, the greater one to govern the day, and the lesser one to govern the night; and he made the stars. God set them in the dome of the sky, to shed light upon the earth, to govern the day and the night, and to separate the light from the darkness. God saw how good it was. Evening came, and morning followed—the fourth day.

Then God said, "Let the water teem with an abundance of living creatures, and on the earth let birds fly beneath the dome of the sky." And so it happened: God created the great sea monsters and all kinds of swimming creatures with which the water teems, and all kinds of winged birds. God saw how good it was, and God blessed them, saying, "Be fertile, multiply, and fill the water of the seas; and let the birds multiply on the earth." Evening came, and morning followed—the fifth day.

Then God said, "Let the earth bring forth all kinds of living creatures: cattle, creeping things, and wild animals of all kinds." And so it happened: God made all kinds of wild animals, all kinds of cattle, and all kinds of creeping things of the earth. God saw how good it was. Then God said: "Let us make man in our image, after our likeness. Let them have dominion over the fish of the sea, the birds of the air, and the cattle, and over all the wild animals and the creatures that crawl on the ground."
God created man in his image;
in the divine image he created him;
male and female he created them.
God blessed them, saying; "Be fertile and multiply; fill the earth and subdue it. Have dominion over the fish of the sea, the birds of the air, and all the living things that move on the earth." God also said: "See, I give you every seed-bearing plant all over the earth and every tree that has seed-bearing fruit on it to be your food; and to all the animals of the land, all the birds of the air, and all the living creatures that crawl on the ground, I give all the green plants for food." And so it happened. God looked at everything he had made, and he found it very good. Evening came, and morning followed—the sixth day.

Thus the heavens and the earth and all their array were completed. Since on the seventh day God was finished with the work he had been doing, he rested on the seventh day from all the work he had undertaken.     Genesis 1:1–2:2

L ORD, send out your Spirit,
  and renew the face of the earth.

Bless the Lord, my soul!
Lord, God, how great you are,
clothed in majesty and glory,
wrapped in light as in a robe!

You founded the earth on its base,
to stand firm from age to age.
You wrapped it with the ocean like a cloak:
the waters stood higher than the mountains.

You make springs gush forth in the valleys;
they flow in between the hills.
On their banks dwell the birds of heaven;
from the branches they sing their song.

From your dwelling you water the hills;
earth drinks its fill of your gift.
You make the grass grow for the cattle
and the plants to serve our needs,
that we may bring forth bread from the earth.

How many are your works, O Lord!
In wisdom you have made them all.
The earth is full of your riches.

From Psalm 104    Bless the Lord, my soul.

THE earth is full
of the goodness of the Lord.

The word of the Lord is faithful
and all his works to be trusted.
The Lord loves justice and right
and fills the earth with his love.

By his word the heavens were made,
by the breath of his mouth all the stars.
He collects the waves of the ocean;
he stores up the depths of the sea.

They are happy, whose God is the Lord,
the people he has chosen as his own.
From the heavens the Lord looks forth,
he sees all the children of earth.

Our soul is waiting for the Lord.
The Lord is our help and our shield.
May your love be upon us, O Lord,
as we place all our hope in you.                    From Psalm 33

ALMIGHTY and eternal God,
you created all things in wonderful
beauty and order.
Help us now to perceive
how still more wonderful is the new creation
by which in the fullness of time
you redeemed your people
through the sacrifice of our passover, Jesus Christ.        Roman rite

L ORD God,
the creation of man was a wonderful work,
his redemption still more wonderful.
May we persevere in right reason
against all that entices to sin

*Roman rite*    and so attain to everlasting joy.

O God, who wonderfully created, and yet more wonderfully restored, the dignity of human nature: Grant that we may share the divine life of him who *The Book of* humbled himself to share our humanity, your Son Jesus *Common Prayer* Christ our Lord.

G OD put Abraham to the test. He called to him, "Abraham!" "Ready!" he replied. Then God said: "Take your son Isaac, your only one, whom you love, and go the land of Moriah. There you shall offer him up as a holocaust on a height that I will point out to you." Early the next morning Abraham saddled his donkey, took with him his son Isaac, and two of his servants as well, and with the wood that he had cut for the holocaust, set out for the place of which God had told him.

On the third day Abraham got sight of the place from afar. Then he said to his servants: "Both of you stay here with the donkey, while the boy and I go on over yonder. We will worship and then come back to you." Thereupon Abraham took the wood for the holocaust and laid it on his son Isaac's shoulders, while he himself carried the fire and the knife. As the two walked on together, Isaac spoke to his father Abraham. "Father!" he said. "Yes, son," he replied. Isaac continued, "Here are the fire and the wood, but where is the sheep for the holocaust?" "Son," Abraham answered, "God himself will provide the sheep for the holocaust." Then the two continued going forward.

When they came to the place of which God had told him, Abraham built an altar there and arranged the wood on it. Next he tied up his son Isaac, and put him on top of the wood on the altar. Then he reached out and took the knife to slaughter his son. But the Lord's messenger called to him from heaven, "Abraham, Abraham!" "Yes, Lord," he answered. "Do not lay your hand on the boy," said the messenger. "Do not do the least thing to him. I know now how devoted you are to God, since you did not withhold from me your own beloved son." As Abraham looked about, he spied a ram caught by its horns in the thicket. So he went and took the ram and offered it up as a holocaust in place of his son. Abraham named the site Yahweh-yireh; hence people now say, "On the mountain the Lord will see."

Again the Lord's messenger called to Abraham from heaven and said: "I swear by myself, declares the Lord, that because you acted as you did in not withholding from me your beloved son, I will bless you abundantly and make your descendants as countless as the stars of the sky and the sands of the seashore; your descendants shall take possession of the gates of their enemies, and in your descendants all the nations of the earth shall find

Genesis 22:1–18    blessing—all this because you obeyed my command."

K EEP me safe, O God;
you are my hope.

O Lord, it is you who are my portion and cup,
it is you yourself who are my prize.
I keep the Lord ever in my sight;
since he is at my right hand, I shall stand firm.

And so my heart rejoices, my soul is glad;
even my body shall rest in safety.
For you will not leave my soul among the dead,
nor let your beloved know decay.

You will show me the path of life,
the fullness of joy in your presence,

From Psalm 16    at your right hand happiness for ever.

G OD and Father of all who believe in you,
you promised Abraham that he would become
the father of all nations,
and through the death and resurrection of Christ
you fulfill that promise:
everywhere throughout the world you increase
      your chosen people.
May we respond to your call
by joyfully accepting your invitation to a new life
      of grace.                                        Roman rite

G OD and Father of all believers, for the glory of your
name multiply, by the grace of the paschal
sacrament, the number of your children; that your church
may rejoice to see fulfilled your promise to our father     *The Book of*
Abraham.                                                    *Common Prayer*

T HE Lord said to Moses, "Why are you crying out to me? Tell the Israelites to go forward. And you, lift up your staff and, with hand outstretched over the sea, split the sea in two, that the Israelites may pass through it on dry land. But I will make the Egyptians so obstinate that they will go in after them. Then I will receive glory through Pharaoh and all his army, his chariots and charioteers. The Egyptians shall know that I am the Lord, when I receive glory through Pharaoh and his chariots and charioteers."

The angel of God, who had been leading Israel's camp, now moved and went around behind them. The column of cloud also, leaving the front, took up its place behind them, so that it came between the camp of the Egyptians and that of Israel. But the cloud now became dark, and thus the night passed without the rival camps coming any closer together all night long. Then Moses stretched out his hand over the sea, and the Lord swept the sea with a strong east wind throughout the night and so turned it into dry land. When the water was thus divided, the Israelites marched into the midst of the sea on dry land, with the water like a wall to their right and to their left.

The Egyptians followed in pursuit; all Pharaoh's horses and chariots and charioteers went after them right into the midst of the sea. In the night watch just before dawn the Lord cast through the column of the fiery cloud upon the Egyptian force a glance that threw it into a panic; and he so clogged their chariot wheels that they could hardly drive. With that the Egyptians sounded the retreat before Israel, because the Lord was fighting for them against the Egyptians.

Then the Lord told Moses, "Stretch out your hand over the sea, that the water may flow back upon the Egyptians, upon their chariots and their charioteers." So Moses stretched out his hand over the sea, and at dawn the sea flowed back to its normal depth. The Egyptians were fleeing head on toward the sea, when the Lord hurled them into its midst. As the water flowed back, it covered the chariots and the charioteers of Pharaoh's whole army

which had followed the Israelites into the sea. Not a single
one of them escaped. But the Israelites had marched on
dry land through the midst of the sea, with the water like a
wall to their right and to their left. Thus the Lord saved
Israel on that day from the power of the Egyptians. When
Israel saw the Egyptians lying dead on the seashore and
beheld the great power that the Lord had shown against
the Egyptians, they feared the Lord and believed in him
and in his servant Moses.

Then Moses and the Israelites sang this song to the Lord:
   I will sing to the Lord, for he is gloriously triumphant;
     horse and chariot he has cast into the sea.          Exodus 14:15–15:1

L ET us sing to the Lord;
  he has covered himself in glory.

I will sing to the Lord, glorious his triumph!
Horse and rider he has thrown into the sea!
The Lord is my strength, my song, my salvation.
This is my God and I extol him,
my parents' God and I give him praise.

The Lord is a warrior! The Lord is his name.
The chariots of Pharaoh he hurled into the sea,
the flower of his army is drowned in the sea.

The deeps hide them; they sank like a stone.
Your right hand, Lord, glorious in its power,
your right hand, Lord, has shattered the enemy.

The people you have redeemed pass by,
you will lead them and plant them on your mountain,
the place, O Lord, where you have made your home,
the sanctuary, Lord, which your hands have made.
The Lord will reign for ever and ever!       From Exodus 15

FATHER, even today we see the wonders
of the miracles you worked long ago.
You once saved a single nation from slavery,
and now you offer that salvation to all through baptism.
May the peoples of the world become true children
      of Abraham
and prove worthy of the heritage of Israel.

Roman rite

LORD God,
in the new covenant
you shed light on the miracles you worked
      in ancient times:
the Red Sea is a symbol of our baptism,
and the nation you freed from slavery
is a sign of your Christian people.
May every nation
share the faith and privilege of Israel
and come to new birth in the Holy Spirit.

Roman rite

HE who has become your husband is your Maker;
his name is the Lord of hosts;
Your redeemer is the Holy One of Israel,
  called God of all the earth.
The Lord calls you back,
  like a wife forsaken and grieved in spirit,
A wife married in youth and then cast off,
  says your God.
For a brief moment I abandoned you,
  but with great tenderness I will take you back.
In an outburst of wrath, for a moment
  I hid my face from you;
But with enduring love I take pity on you,
  says the Lord, your redeemer.
This is for me like the days of Noah,
  when I swore that the waters of Noah
  should never again deluge the earth;
So I have sworn not to be angry with you,
  or to rebuke you.
Though the mountains leave their place
  and the hills be shaken,
My love shall never leave you
  nor my covenant of peace be shaken,
  says the Lord, who has mercy on you.
O afflicted one, storm-battered and unconsoled,
  I lay your pavements in carnelians,
  and your foundations in sapphires;
I will make your battlements of rubies,
  your gates of carbuncles,
  and all your walls of precious stones.
All your sons shall be taught by the Lord,
  and great shall be the peace of your children.
In justice shall you be established,
  far from the fear of oppression,
  where destruction cannot come near you.    Isaiah 54:5–14

I will praise you, Lord,
for you have rescued me.

I will praise you, Lord, you have rescued me
and have not let my enemies rejoice over me.
O Lord, you have raised my soul from the dead,
restored me to life from those who sink into the grave.

Sing psalms to the Lord, you who love him
give thanks to his holy name.
His anger lasts a moment; his favor all through life.
At night there are tears, but joy comes with dawn.

The Lord listened and had pity.
The Lord came to my help.
For me you have changed my mourning into dancing.
From Psalm 30    O Lord my God, I will thank you for ever.

ALMIGHTY and eternal God,
glorify your name by increasing
your chosen people
as you promised long ago.
In reward for their trust,
may we see in the church the fulfillment
Roman rite        of your promise.

THUS says the Lord:
   All you who are thirsty,
   come to the water!
You who have no money,
   come, receive grain and eat;
Come, without paying and without cost,
   drink wine and milk!
Why spend your money for what is not bread;
   your wages for what fails to satisfy?
Heed me, and you shall eat well,
   you shall delight in rich fare.
Come to me heedfully,
   listen, that you may have life.
I will renew with you the everlasting covenant,
   the benefits assured to David.
As I made him a witness to the peoples,
   a leader and commander of nations,
So shall you summon a nation you knew not,
   and nations that knew you not shall run to you,
Because of the Lord, your God,
   the Holy One of Israel, who has glorified you.
Seek the Lord while he may be found,
   call him while he is near.
Let the scoundrel forsake his way,
   and the wicked man his thoughts;
Let him turn to the Lord for mercy;
   to our God, who is generous in forgiving.
For my thoughts are not your thoughts,
   nor are your ways my ways, says the Lord.
As high as the heavens are above the earth,
   so high are my ways above your ways
   and my thoughts above your thoughts.
For just as from the heavens
   the rain and snow come down

And do not return there
   till they have watered the earth,
   making it fertile and fruitful,
Giving seed to him who sows
   and bread to him who eats,
So shall my word be
   that goes forth from my mouth;
It shall not return to me void,
   but shall do my will,
Isaiah 55:1–11   achieving the end for which I sent it.

YOU will draw water joyfully
   from the springs of salvation.

Truly, God is my salvation, I trust, I shall not fear.
For the Lord is my strength, my song, he became
   my savior.
With joy you will draw water from the wells
   of salvation.

Give thanks to the Lord, give praise to his name!
Make his mighty deeds known to the peoples!
Declare the greatness of his name.

Sing a psalm to the Lord!
For he has done glorious deeds,
   make them known to all the earth!
People of Sion, sing and shout for joy
From Isaiah 12   for great in your midst is the Holy One of Israel.

ALMIGHTY, ever-living God,
  only hope of the world,
by the preaching of the prophets
you proclaimed the mysteries we are celebrating
      tonight.
Help us to be your faithful people,
for it is by your inspiration alone
that we can grow in goodness.                    Roman rite

O God, you have created all things by the power of
  your word, and you renew the earth by your Spirit:
Give now the water of life to those who thirst for you, that
they may bring forth abundant fruit in your glorious     The Book of
kingdom.                                                 Common Prayer

H EAR, O Israel, the commandments of life:
 listen, and know prudence!
How is it, Israel,
  that you are in the land of your foes,
  grown old in a foreign land,
Defiled with the dead,
  accounted with those destined for the nether world?
You have forsaken the fountain of wisdom!
  Had you walked in the way of God,
  you would have dwelt in enduring peace.
Learn where prudence is,
  where strength, where understanding;
That you may know also
  where are the length of days, and life,
  where light of the eyes, and peace.

Who has found the place of wisdom,
  who has entered into her treasuries?
He who knows all things knows her;
  he has probed her by his knowledge—
He who established the earth for all time,
  and filled it with four-footed beasts;
He who dismisses the light, and it departs,
  calls it, and it obeys him trembling;
Before whom the stars at their posts
  shine and rejoice;
When he calls them, they answer, "Here we are!"
  shining with joy for their Maker.
Such is our God;
  no other is to be compared to him:
He has traced out all the way of understanding,
  and has given her to Jacob, his servant,
  to Israel, his beloved son.

Since then she has appeared on earth,
  and moved among men.
She is the book of the precepts of God,
  the law that endures forever;
All who cling to her will live,
  but those will die who forsake her.
Turn, O Jacob, and receive her:
  walk by her light toward splendor.
Give not your glory to another,
  your privileges to an alien race.
Blessed are we, O Israel;
  for what pleases God is known to us!                Baruch 3:9–15, 32–4:4

L ORD,
you have the words of everlasting life.

The law of the Lord is perfect,
it revives the soul.
The rule of the Lord is to be trusted,
it gives wisdom to the simple.

The precepts of the Lord are right,
they gladden the heart.
The command of the Lord is clear,
it gives light to the eyes.

The fear of the Lord is holy,
abiding for ever.
The decrees of the Lord are truth
and all of them just.

They are more to be desired than gold,
than the purest of gold
and sweeter are they than honey,

From Psalm 19   than honey from the comb.

F ATHER,
you increase your church
by continuing to call all people to salvation.
Listen to our prayers

Roman rite   and always watch over those you cleanse in baptism.

THUS the word of the Lord came to me: Son of man, when the house of Israel lived in their land, they defiled it by their conduct and deeds. In my sight their conduct was like the defilement of a menstruous woman. Therefore I poured out my fury upon them [because of the blood which they poured out on the ground, and because they defiled it with idols]. I scattered them among the nations, dispersing them over foreign lands; according to their conduct and deeds I judged them. But when they came among the nations [wherever they came], they served to profane my holy name, because it was said of them: "These are the people of the Lord, yet they had to leave their land." So I have relented because of my holy name which the house of Israel profaned among the nations where they came. Therefore say to the house of Israel: Thus says the Lord God: Not for your sakes do I act, house of Israel, but for the sake of my holy name, which you profaned among the nations to which you came. I will prove the holiness of my great name, profaned among the nations, in whose midst you have profaned it. Thus the nations shall know that I am the Lord, says the Lord God, when in their sight I prove my holiness through you. For I will take you away from among the nations, gather you from all the foreign lands, and bring you back to your own land. I will sprinkle clean water upon you to cleanse you from all your impurities, and from all your idols I will cleanse you. I will give you a new heart and place a new spirit within you, taking from your bodies your stony hearts and giving you natural hearts. I will put my spirit within you and make you live by my statutes, careful to observe my decrees. You shall live in the land I gave your fathers; you shall be my people, and I will be your God.    Ezekiel 36:16-28

CREATE a clean heart in me,
O God.

A pure heart create for me, O God,
put a steadfast spirit within me.
Do not cast me away from your presence,
nor deprive me of your holy spirit.

Give me again the joy of your help;
with a spirit of fervor sustain me,
that I may teach transgressors your ways
and sinners may return to you.

For in sacrifice you take no delight,
burnt offering from me you would refuse;
my sacrifice, a contrite spirit,
From Psalm 51   a humbled, contrite heart you will not spurn.

GOD of unchanging power and light,
look with mercy and favor on your entire church.
Bring lasting salvation to humankind,
so that the world may see
the fallen lifted up,
the old made new,
and all things brought to perfection,
through him who is their origin,
Roman rite   our Lord Jesus Christ.

F ATHER,
you teach us in both the Old and the New Testament
to celebrate this passover mystery.
Help us to understand your great love for us.
May the goodness you now show us
confirm our hope in your future mercy.                    Roman rite

A LMIGHTY and eternal God,
be present in this sacrament of your love.
Send your Spirit of adoption
on those to be born again in baptism.
And may the work of our humble ministry
be brought to perfection by your mighty power.            Roman rite

A LMIGHTY and everlasting God, who in the paschal
mystery established the new covenant of
reconciliation: Grant that all who are reborn into the
fellowship of Christ's body may show forth in their lives     *The Book of*
what they profess by their faith.                             *Common Prayer*

ALMIGHTY God, you have placed in the skies the sign of
your covenant with all living things: Grant that we,
who are saved through water and the Spirit, may worthily
offer to you our sacrifice of thanksgiving.

After Genesis 7–9
*The Book of*
*Common Prayer*

ALMIGHTY God, by the passover of your Son you have
brought us out of sin into righteousness and out of
death into life: Grant to those who are sealed by your
Holy Spirit the will and the power to proclaim you to all
the world.

After Ezekiel 37
*The Book of*
*Common Prayer*

O God of unchangeable power and eternal light:
Look favorably on your whole church, that
wonderful and sacred mystery; by the effectual working of
your providence, carry out in tranquility the plan of
salvation; let the whole world see and know that things
which were cast down are being raised up, and things
which had grown old are being made new, and that all
things are being brought to their perfection by him
through whom all things are made, your Son Jesus Christ
our Lord.

After Zephaniah 3
*The Book of*
*Common Prayer*

O God, by the word of the prophets you are known in the church as the sower of the good seed, the keeper of the chosen vineyard. Grant to your people who are called your vine and your harvest, that, cleansed of all thorns and briars, they may abundantly bring forth good fruit.

*After Isaiah 4*
*Lutheran Book*
*of Worship*

O God, you have united all nations in the confession of your name. Now give us the will and the power to do what you command, that the faith of the people whom you call to everlasting life may direct their speech and actions.

*After Jonah 3*
*Lutheran Book*
*of Worship*

L ORD God,
you have brightened this night
with the radiance of the risen Christ.
Quicken the spirit of sonship in your church;
renew us in mind and body
to give you whole-hearted service.

*Roman rite*

O God, who made this most holy night to shine with the glory of the Lord's resurrection: Stir up in your church that spirit of adoption which is given to us in baptism, that we, being renewed both in body and mind, may worship you in sincerity and truth.

*The Book of*
*Common Prayer*

A RE you not aware that we who were baptized into Christ Jesus were baptized into his death? Through baptism into his death we were buried with him, so that, just as Christ was raised from the dead by the glory of the Father, we too might live a new life. If we have been united with him through likeness to his death, so shall we be through a like resurrection. This we know: our old self was crucified with him so that the sinful body might be destroyed and we might be slaves to sin no longer. A man who is dead has been freed from sin. If we have died with Christ, we believe that we are also to live with him. We know that Christ, once raised from the dead, will never die again; death has no more power over him. His death was death to sin, once for all; his life is life for God. In the same way, you must consider yourselves dead to sin but alive for God in Christ Jesus.

Romans 6:3–11

A LLELUIA, alleluia, alleluia!

Give thanks to the Lord for he is good,
for his love has no end.
Let the children of Israel say:
"His love has no end."

The Lord's right hand has triumphed;
his right hand raised me.
The Lord's right hand has triumphed;
I shall not die, I shall live
and recount his deeds.

The stone which the builders rejected
has become the corner stone.
This is the work of the Lord,
a marvel in our eyes.

From Psalm 118

L ET us chant Alleluia. Then the word of scripture will be accomplished, the word not of combatants any more, but of victors; *Death has been swallowed up in victory.*

Let us chant Alleluia. *O Death, where is your sting?*

Let us chant Alleluia. *The sting of death is sin* (1 Cor 15:56). *You will seek its place and will not find it* (Psalm 37:10).

Let us chant Alleluia here in the midst of dangers and temptations, we and the others. *God is faithful,* says the apostle, *he will not allow us to be tempted above our ability* (1 Cor 10:13).

O blessed Alleluia of heaven! No more anguish, no more adversity. No more enemy. No more love of destruction. Up above, praise to God, and here below, praise to God. Praise mingled with fear here, but without disturbance above. Here the one who chants must die, but there he will live for ever. Here we chant in hope, there, in possession; here it is Alleluia *en route,* there it is Alleluia on arriving home.

Augustine
Fifth century

A FTER the sabbath, as the first day of the week was dawning, Mary Magdalene came with the other Mary to inspect the tomb. Suddenly there was a mighty earthquake, as the angel of the Lord descended from heaven. He came to the stone, rolled it back, and sat on it. In appearance he resembled a flash of lightning while his garments were as dazzling as snow. The guards grew paralyzed with fear of him and fell down like dead men. Then the angel spoke, addressing the women: "Do not be frightened. I know you are looking for Jesus the crucified, but he is not here. He has been raised, exactly as he promised. Come and see the spot where he was laid. Then go quickly and tell his disciples: 'He has been raised from the dead and now goes ahead of you to Galilee, where you will see him.' That is the message I have for you."

They hurried away from the tomb half-overjoyed, half-fearful, and ran to carry the good news to his disciples. Suddenly, without warning, Jesus stood before them and said, "Peace!" The women came up and embraced his feet and did him homage. At this Jesus said to them, "Do not be afraid! Go and carry the news to my brothers that they are to go to Galilee, where they will see me."

Matthew 28:1–10
Cycle A, Roman rite

W HEN the sabbath was over, Mary Magdalene, Mary the mother of James, and Salome bought perfumed oils with which they intended to go and anoint Jesus. Very early, just after sunrise, on the first day of the week they came to the tomb. They were saying to one another, "Who will roll back the stone for us from the entrance to the tomb?" When they looked, they found that the stone had been rolled back. (It was a huge one.) On entering the tomb they saw a young man sitting at the right, dressed in a white robe. This frightened them thoroughly, but he reassured them: "You need not be amazed! You are looking for Jesus of Nazareth, the one who was crucified. He has been raised up; he is not here. See the place where they laid him. Go now and tell his disciples and Peter, 'He is going ahead of you to Galilee, where you will see him just as he told you.' " They made their way out and fled from the tomb bewildered and trembling; and because of their great fear, they said nothing to anyone.

Mark 16:1–8
Cycle B, Roman rite

O N the first day of the week, at dawn, the women came to the tomb bringing the spices they had prepared. They found the stone rolled back from the tomb; but when they entered the tomb, they did not find the body of the Lord Jesus. While they were still at a loss what to think of this, two men in dazzling garments appeared beside them. Terrified, the women bowed to the ground. The men said to them: "Why do you search for the living One among the dead? He is not here; he has been raised up. Remember what he said to you while he was still in Galilee—that the Son of Man must be delivered into the hands of sinful men, and be crucified, and on the third day rise again." With this reminder, his words came back to them.

On their return from the tomb, they told all these things to the Eleven and the others. The women were Mary of Magdala, Joanna, and Mary the mother of James. The other women with them also told the apostles, but the story seemed like nonsense and they refused to believe them. Peter, however, got up and ran to the tomb. He stooped down but could see nothing but the wrappings. So he went away full of amazement at what had occurred.

Luke 24:1–12
Cycle C, Roman rite

L ET all the pious and all lovers of God rejoice in the splendor of this feast; let the wise servants blissfully enter into the joy of their Lord; let those who have borne the burden of Lent now receive their pay, and those who have toiled since the first hour, let them now receive their due reward; let any who came after the third hour be grateful to join in the feast, and those who may have come after the sixth, let them not be afraid of being too late, for the Lord is gracious and he receives the last even as the first. He gives rest to those who come on the eleventh hour as well as to those who have toiled since the first: yes, he has pity on the last and he serves the first; he rewards the one and is generous to the other; he repays the deed and praises the effort.

Come you all: enter into the joy of your Lord. You the first and you the last, receive alike your reward; you rich and you poor, dance together; you sober and you weaklings, celebrate the day; you who have kept the fast and you who have not, rejoice today. The table is richly loaded: enjoy its royal banquet. The calf is a fatted one: let no one go away hungry. All of you enjoy the banquet of faith; all of you receive the riches of his goodness.

Let none grieve over their poverty, for the universal kingdom has been revealed; let none weep over their sins, for pardon has shone from the grave; let none fear death, for the death of our Savior has set us free: he has destroyed it by enduring it, he has despoiled Hades by going down into its kingdom, he has angered it by allowing it to taste of his flesh.

When Isaiah foresaw all this, he cried out: "O Hades, you have been angered by encountering him in the nether world." Hades is angered because frustrated, it is angered because it has been mocked, it is angered because it has been destroyed, it is angered because it has been reduced to naught, it is angered because it is now captive. It seized a body, and, lo! it discovered God; it seized earth, and, behold! it encountered heaven; it seized the visible, and was overcome by the invisible.

O death, where is your sting? O Hades, where is your victory? Christ is risen and you are abolished, Christ is risen and the demons are cast down, Christ is risen and the angels rejoice, Christ is risen and life is freed, Christ is risen and the tomb is emptied of the dead: for Christ, being risen from the dead, has become the Leader and Reviver of those who had fallen asleep. To him be glory and power for ever and ever.

John Chrysostom
Fifth century

I T is the Lord who made heaven and earth, who in the beginning formed humanity, who was announced by Law and prophets, who was incarnate in a virgin, who was suspended from the wood. Buried in the earth, he was raised from the dead and ascended into the heights and is now seated at the right hand of the Father and has the power to judge and the power to save all.

Through him the Father made that which has been made from the beginning and even unto ages unending: alpha and omega, beginning and end—beginning inexpressible, ending incomprehensible—Christ, King, Jesus, Captain, Lord, risen from the dead, sitting at the right hand of the Father—in the Father, the Father in him—to him be glory and power forever.

Melito of Sardis
Second century

CRISTES pepull, bothe men and woymen, as ye all knowen wele, thys day is called in sum place Astyr-day, and in sum plase Pase-day, and in sum plas Godis Sonday.

Hyt is called Astyr-day . . . for wel nygh in ych plase, hyt ys the maner thys day forto do fyre out of the hall at the astyr, that hathe all the wyntyr brent wyth fyre and blakyd wyth smoke. Hit shall thys day ben arayde wyth grene rusches, and swete flowres strawed all aboute, scheyng an hegh ensampull to all men and woymen that, rhght as thay maken clene the howse all wythyn, beryng out the fure and strawyng flowres, ryyt so ye schull clanse the howse of your soule, doyng away the fyre of lechery and of dedly wrath and of envy, and straw ther swete erbes and flowres; and that ben vertues of goodnes and of mekenes, of kyndnes, of love and charite, of pes and of rest: and soo make the howse of your soule abull to receyve your God. . . . And rhght as ye clothuth your astyr of your soule, that is, your hert, in fayr clothe of charyte, and of love, and of pes, and of rest wyth all Godys pepull, that ye mow abull be forto recyve the best frende that ye have, that is Crist, Godys sonne of Heven, that thys tyme suffred dethe, forto bryng you to the lyfe that ever shall last.

This day is also callyd Pase-day, that is in Englysch, the passyng day. . . . Ych Godys chyld shall passe out of evell levyng into good lyvyng, out of vyccs, ynto vertuys, out of pride into mekenes, out of covetyse into largenes, out of sloth into holy bysynes, out of envy into love and charite, out of wrathe into mercy, out of gloteny into abstynens, out of lechery into chastyte, out of the fendys clochus ynto Godys barm; and soo of Godys enmy make hys frende and derlyng. Whosoe passythe thus, is worthy forto come to that gret fest that God makythe thys day to all that thys passage makut.

This day ys called Godis Sonday; for Crist, Godis sonne of Heven, thys day roos from deth to lyve, and soo gladyth all hys servantes and frendys. . . . Wherfor all holy chrych makythe myrth thys day and syngyth thus: "This ys the day that our Lord made; be we glad and ioyfull in hure!" The Fadyr of Heven makyth wyth all hys angelys soo gret melody for the vpryst of hys sonne, that he makythe thys day a gret passyng fest, and byddythe all hys pepull therto, als wele hom that ben in Heven as thylke that ben in erthe.

*From an early English text for preachers Fourteenth century*

T HE text of the Hebrew Exodus has been read and the words of the mystery have been explained: how the sheep was sacrificed for the salvation of the people.

For born Son-like, and led forth lamb-like, and slaughtered sheep-like, and buried human-like, he has risen God-like, being by nature God and human.

He is all things: in as much as he judges, Law; in as much as he teaches, Word; in as much as he saves, Grace; in as much as he begets, Father; in as much as he is begotten, Son; in as much as he suffers, sheep; in as much as he is buried, human; in as much as he has risen, God.

*Melito of Sardis Second century*

This is Jesus Christ to whom be glory for ever and ever. Amen.

THE water is to be water flowing from a fountain, or running water. This rule is to be observed except when impossible. . . .

The candidates are to remove their clothes.

The children are to be baptized first. All of them who can are to give answer for themselves. If they cannot, let their parents or someone in the family answer for them. . . .

Let no one go down into the water with anything of the stranger.

The priest will take aside each of those who are to receive baptism. He will order each to turn to the west and to make abjuration in these words: "I renounce you, Satan, and all your undertakings, and all your works."

After this abjuration, he anoints them with the oil of exorcism, saying: "Let every evil spirit depart from you!"

A deacon descends into the water with the one to be baptized. . . . The one doing the baptizing lays his hand on the person and asks:
    Do you believe in God, the Father almighty?
The one being baptized is to answer: "I believe." Let him baptize the person a first time, keeping his hand on the head of the one being baptized. He then asks:
    Do you believe in Christ Jesus, Son of God,
    born by the Holy Spirit of the Virgin Mary,
    who was crucified under Pontius Pilate,
    who died, was raised on the third day,
    living from among the dead,
    who ascended to the heavens,
    who will come to judge the living and the dead?
When the person has answered: "I believe," he is to baptize the person a second time. He is to ask again:
    Do you believe in the Holy Spirit,
    in the holy church,
    in the resurrection of the flesh?
The one being baptized is to answer: "I believe." Then he baptizes a third time.

After this, the priest will anoint the person with the oil of thanksgiving. He will say: "I anoint you with the oil that has been sanctified in the name of Jesus Christ." After drying themselves off, they will put their clothes on again and enter the church.

*This account of the church's practice at the beginning of the third century in Rome continues with the anointing of the newly baptized.*

With his hand [the bishop] next pours the oil of thanksgiving. He spreads it on their heads, saying: "I anoint you with the holy oil in the Lord, Father almighty, Christ Jesus and the Holy Spirit."

He will then mark them with the sign on the forehead, then give them a kiss, saying: "The Lord is with you." The person marked with the sign will answer: "And with your spirit." He is to do this for each one.

From now on they will pray with the entire people. But they are not to pray with the faithful before receiving all this. When they have prayed, let them offer the kiss of peace.

*Finally, the eucharist of the Vigil is described.*

[The bishop] gives thanks with regard to the bread, which represents the body of Christ; also with regard to the cup, in which the wine is mixed that represents the blood poured out for all those who believe in him. He also gives thanks with regard to the mingled milk and honey, which represents the fulfillment of the promise God made to our ancestors, a promise signified by the land flowing with milk and honey and fulfilled in the flesh of Christ which he gives us and by which believers are nourished like little children, for the sweetness of his word changes the bitterness of our hearts into gentleness. Finally, he gives thanks with regard to the water for the oblation, to signify purification, so that the interior, spiritual person may receive the same effect as the body. . . .

After breaking the bread, he distributes each piece, saying: "The bread of heaven in Christ Jesus!"
The person receiving it is to answer: "Amen."

Those who drink will taste each cup. . . . When all this is finished, each person must hasten to do good works, please God, and live a good life. Let them devote themselves to the church, putting into practice what they have been taught and making progress in the service of God.

*The Apostolic Tradition*
Hippolytus
Third century

T HEN the liturgy is sung. In the litany some names of saints may be added, especially the titular of the church, the local patrons and the saints of those to be baptized.

Roman rite

*As suggested by the rubric, the names of other saints have been added in the following list.*

Mary, Mother of God    Michael    Gabriel    Raphael

Adam    Eve    Abel    Enoch    Noah    Abraham

Sarah    Isaac    Rebekah    Jacob    Rachel    Judah

Joseph    Benjamin    Moses    Miriam    Aaron

Joshua    Deborah    Gideon    Samson    Naomi    Ruth

Hannah    Samuel    Saul    Jonathan    David

Abigail    Solomon    Nathan    Elijah    Elisha    Hosea

Amos    Isaiah    Micah    Jeremiah    Ezra    Joel

Nehemiah    Daniel    Esther    Judith    Joseph    Anna

Simeon    Zachariah    Elizabeth    John the Baptist

Peter    Paul    Andrew    John    James    Thomas

Matthew    Philip    Bartholomew    Simon    Martha

Mary    Mary Magdalene    Joanna    Matthias

Stephen    Barnabas    Mark    Timothy    Lydia

Clement    Polycarp    Cecelia    Perpetua    Felicity

Agatha    Barbara    Lawrence    Blase

Cosmas and Damian    Lucy    Irene    George    Agnes

Ursula    Boniface    Eric    Wenceslaus    Stanislaus

Thomas Becket    Thomas More    Oliver Plunket

Isaac Jogues    Kateri Tekakwitha    Charles Lwanga

Maximilian Kolbe    Francis de Sales    Patrick

Martin of Tours    Nicholas    Leo    Gregory    Anselm

John Neumann    Anthony    Benedict    Scholastica

Brendon    Hilda    Edith    Bernard    Norbert

Francis    Clare    Dominic    Gertrude    Rita

Ignatius of Loyola    Elizabeth Ann Seton    Basil

Cyril of Jerusalem    Ambrose    John Chrysostom

Augustine    Jerome    Albert    Thomas Aquinas

Catherine of Siena    Teresa    John of the Cross    Helen

Emily    Monica    Henry    Margaret    Isidore

Louis    Bridget    Joan    Angela    Jane de Chantal

Peter Claver    Martin de Porres    Rose

Vincent de Paul    Louise de Marillac    Theresa

John Vianney    Bernadette    Frances Cabrini

D O you reject sin so as to live in the freedom of God's children?

Do you reject the glamor of evil and refuse to be mastered by sin?

Do you reject Satan, father of sin and prince of darkness?

N., do you believe in God, the Father almighty, creator of heaven and earth?

Do you believe in Jesus Christ, his only Son, our Lord, who was born of the Virgin Mary, was crucified, died, and was buried, rose from the dead, and is now seated at the right hand of the Father?

Do you believe in the Holy Spirit, the holy catholic church, the communion of saints, the forgiveness of sins, the resurrection of the body, and life everlasting?          Roman rite

T HE renunciation of the devil must have been adopted in all the churches prior to Nicaea. . . . The North African church in Tertullian's day had: "I renounce the devil, his pomp, and his angels." Ambrose's church in Milan had the candidate renounce, "the devil and his works, the world, its luxuries and pleasures." In Gaul, the renunciation included, "the devil, the world, and sins." According to Chrysostom, at Antioch it was: "I renounce you, Satan, and your pomp, and your service," and at Constantinople, "I renounce you, and your pomps, and your service, and your angels."

The renunciation was very personal: Satan is addressed directly as if he were present and visible—he is defied "to his face," by having the candidate face the west during the renunciation, a custom apparently universal by the fourth century. . . . In many places hands were outstretched towards the west, "toward the devil," "as though he were present himself." In some churches the candidates were even made to spit toward the west.          Casimir Kucharek

*The priest turns the person to face the west, unclad, unshod, and having hands uplifted.*

DO you renounce Satan, and all his angels, and all his works, and all his service, and all his pride?

Have you renounced Satan?

Breathe and spit upon him.

*The priest then turns the person to face the east, with hands lowered.*

Do you unite yourself to Christ?

Have you united yourself to Christ?

Do you believe in him?

I believe in him as King and as God.

Orthodox liturgy

TO renounce Satan thus is not to reject a mythological being in whose existence one does not even believe. It is to reject an entire worldview made up of pride and self-affirmation, of that pride which has truly taken human life from God and made it into darkness, death and hell. And one can be sure that Satan will not forget this renunciation, this rejection, this challenge. "Breathe and spit upon him!" A war is declared! A fight begins whose real issue is either eternal life or eternal damnation. For this is what Christianity is about! This is what our choice ultimately means!

Alexander Schmemann

DEAR and true children of the church, I have long desired to instruct you in these spiritual and heavenly mysteries of the church . . . so that you may know the work that has been done in you on this evening of your baptism.

First, you entered the vestibule of the baptistry and, standing there, you listened while facing the west. Then they bade you raise your hand, and you renounced Satan, as if he were actually present. . . . [Just as] the tyrant pursued the people of the old as far as the sea, this shameless, impudent demon, the source of all evil, pursues you as far as the fountain of salvation. The tyrant was submerged in the sea; the demon disappears in the waters of salvation.

That is why you were ordered to raise your hand and say to Satan, as if he were actually present: "I renounce you, Satan."

What did you say say then, each of you, as you stood there? "I renounce you, Satan, wicked and cruel tyrant!" And you asserted: "Henceforth, I am no longer in your power. For Christ destroyed that power by sharing with me a nature of flesh and blood. He destroyed death by dying; never again shall I be enslaved to you. I renounce you, crafty serpent full of deceit! I renounce you who lurk in ambush, who pretend friendship but have been the cause of every iniquity, who instigated the sin of our first parents! I renounce you, Satan, author and abettor of every evil."

When you renounce Satan, you break off every agreement you have entered into with him, every covenant you have established with hell. Then there opens to you the paradise which God planted in the east and from which disobedience expelled our first parents. It is in order to symbolize this that you turn from the west to the east, the land of light. Then they asked you to declare yourself: "I believe in the Father, in the Son, in the Holy Spirit, and in a single baptism of repentance."

Draw strength from the words you spoke and be watchful. For, as we have just read, your adversary, the devil, prowls like a roaring lion, seeking whom he may devour. Formerly death was powerful and could devour. But in the bath of new birth God has dried all the tears from every face. Never again shall you weep; you shall always be on holiday, for you have put on the garment of salvation, Jesus Christ.

As soon as you entered [the baptistry], you stripped off your tunic. This rite signified the stripping off of the old self with all its activities.

Stripped of your garments you were naked and thus resembled Christ on the cross. There, by his nakedness, Christ despoiled the Principalities and Powers and, by means of the wood, dragged them after him in his triumphal procession. Now, since the hostile powers were hiding in your members, you could no longer be allowed to wear this shabby tunic. I am speaking, of course, not of the garment people see but of the old self that is being corrupted by the lusts that lead astray. May the soul that has stripped off that garment once and for all not put it on again! Let it say, rather, as the Spouse of Christ says in the Song of Songs: "I have stripped off my tunic, how shall I put it on again?" What a marvelous thing! You were naked in the sight of all, yet you did not blush. In very truth, you were an image of the first man, Adam, who in the garden was likewise naked and did not blush.

Stripped of your garments, you were anointed from the crown of your head to your feet with the oil of exorcism. Here you became a sharer in the true olive tree and grafted on to the true olive tree, and therefore you share in the anointing that the true olive tree bestows. For the oil over which an exorcism has been spoken symbolizes our sharing in the anointing of Christ. It removes all the marks left by the hostile power. Just as the insufflations by the saints [breathing on the catechumens by members of the church] and the invocation of the name of God burn like the hottest flame and put the demons to flight, so this oil of exorcism acquires a marvelous power, thanks to the invocation of God's name and the prayer. Not only does it purify all the traces of sin by burning them away, but it also puts to flight the invisible powers of the Evil One.

Cyril of Jerusalem
Fourth century

A FTER that, as night approaches, [the priest] removes all your clothing, and as though meaning to introduce you to heaven itself through the things that are done, he prepares your whole body with an unction of the spiritual oil, so that all your members may be fortified by the unction and defended against the darts of the enemy. After the unction he makes you go down into the sacred waters.

John Chrysostom
Fifth century

A threefold symbolism appears [in stripping]: putting off the old person and old deeds; imitating Christ who died naked on the cross; and Adam naked in paradise without being ashamed.

Casimir Kucharek

B APTISM'S knowledge of Christ is not that of the dining room but of the bath house. It is not a mannered knowledge, for manners, etiquette, and artifice fall away with one's clothes. It is a knowledge of appalling candor, hearty and intimate, less intellectual than physical—as when lovers are said to ''know'' one another. It is more the inspired wisdom of Solomon's Song than of Paul's letter to the Romans. God speaks not only in logic but in the aroma and feel of oil and warm water on the skin, and these too possess their own sort of rigorous logic.

Aidan Kavanagh

O Master, who love men and women
and who love souls,
God of mercy, pity and truth,
we call on you for those who come to follow you,
and we entrust them to the promises of your only
    begotten Son,
who said: "Whose sins you shall forgive,
they shall be forgiven them."
We mark with this anointing these men and women
who present themselves for this divine regeneration.

We beseech our Lord Jesus Christ
to give them the power that heals and strengthens.

Let him manifest himself through this anointing,
let him remove from body, soul, or spirit
every sign of sin, of iniquity,
or the devil's action.

You who love humankind, Benefactor,
Savior of all who turn to you:
Be gracious to these servants of yours;
let your right hand lead them to regeneration.
Let your only-begotten Son, the Word,
bring them to the font.
Let their new birth be honored,
let your grace not be fruitless.
Let your holy Word be at their side,
let your Holy Spirit be with them,
let him repel and put to flight every temptation.

Serapion
Fourth century

L IKE the deer that yearns
for running streams,
so my soul is yearning
for you, my God.

My soul is thirsting for God,
the God of my life;
when can I enter and see
the face of God?

My tears have become my bread,
by night, by day,
as I hear it said all the day long:
"Where is your God?"

These things will I remember
as I pour out my soul:
how I would lead the rejoicing crowd
into the house of God,
amid cries of gladness and thanksgiving,
the throng wild with joy.

Why are you cast down, my soul,
why groan within me?
Hope in God; I will praise him still,
my savior and my God.

My soul is cast down within me
as I think of you,
from the country of Jordan and Mount Hermon,
from the Hill of Mizar.

Deep is calling on deep,
in the roar of waters:
your torrents and all your waves
swept over me.

By day the Lord will send
his loving kindness;
by night I will sing to him,
praise the God of my life.

I will say to God, my rock:
"Why have you forgotten me?
Why do I go mourning
oppressed by the foe?"

With cries that pierce me to the heart,
my enemies revile me,
saying to me all the day long:
"Where is your God?"

Why are you cast down, my soul,
why groan within me?
Hope in God; I will praise him still,
my savior and my God.

Psalm 42
Chant for procession
to the font
Western liturgies

FROM this noble spring a saving water gushes,
which cleanses all human defilement.
Do you wish to know the benefits of the sacred water?
These streams give the faith that regenerates.
Wash away the defilement of your past life
in the sacred fountain.
Surpassing joy to share in the life the water brings!
Whoever resorts to this spring abandons earthly things
and tramples under foot the works of darkness.

Baptistry inscription
St. Lawrence
in Damaso

THE brood born here to live in heaven has life
from water and the fructifying Spirit.
Sinner, seek your cleansing in this stream
that takes the old and gives a new person back.
No barrier can divide where life unites:
one faith, one fount, one Spirit make one people.
A virgin still, the church gives birth to children
conceived of God, delivered in the water.
Washed in this bath the stains will float away
that mark the guilt of Adam and your own.
The stream that flows below sprang
        from the wounded Christ
to wash the whole world clean and give it life.
Children of the water, think no more of earth;
heaven will give you joy; in heaven hope.
Think not your sins too many or too great:
birth in this stream is birth to holiness.

Baptistry inscription
St. John Lateran
Fifth century

ETERNAL Lord, you know all things that are hidden. We
beseech you and implore you: Send your holy power
over this water and sanctify it. Transform it and bless it
against every hostile action, against all magic and
enchantment. Bless those who drink it, as well as those
who sprinkle it on themselves, and those who use it in any
other manner. Grant that it be healing and life for those
who receive it to the glory of your only Son, for yours is
the glory and the power, with the Holy Spirit, for ever and
ever. Amen.

Ancient exorcism
of water

KING and Lord of all things,
Creator of the universe,
through the incarnation of your only-begotten Son,
    Jesus Christ,
you have given to all created nature the grace
    of salvation;
you redeemed your creation
through the coming of your unutterable Word.
Look down now from the height of heaven
and cast your eyes on these waters,
fill them with the Holy Spirit.

Let your unutterable Word be in them,
let him transform their power.
Let him give them the power to be fruitful,
let him fill them with your grace,
so that the mystery which is to be accomplished
may bear fruit in those who will be regenerated
and may fill with your divine grace
all those who go down
and are baptized.

You who love humankind, be gracious,
take pity on those you have created,
Save your creation, the work of your right hand.
Transform all those who are going to be reborn
with your divine and indescribable beauty.
Transfigured and regenerated,
let them thus be saved
and judged worthy of your kingdom.

Serapion
Fourth century

G REAT are you, O Lord, and marvellous are your works, and there is no word which suffices to hymn your wonders.

For you, of your own good will, have brought into being all things which before were not, and by your might you uphold creation, and by your providence you order the world. When you joined together the universe out of four elements, you crowned the circle of the year with four seasons. Before you tremble all the Powers endowed with intelligence. The sun sings to you. The moon glorifies you. The stars meet together before your presence. The light obeys you. The deeps tremble before you. The water-springs are subject to you. You have spread out the heavens as it were a curtain. You have established the earth upon the waters. You have set round about the sea barriers of sand. You have shed abroad the air for breathing. The angelic Powers serve you. The many-eyed Cherubim and the six-winged Seraphim, as they stand round about and fly, veil their faces in awe before your ineffable glory. For you, God inexpressible, existing uncreated before the ages, and ineffable, descended upon earth, and took on the semblance of a servant, and were made in the likeness of humanity: for, because of the tender compassion of your mercy, O Master, you could not endure to behold humanity oppressed by the Devil, but you came and saved us. We confess your grace. We proclaim your mercy. We conceal not your gracious acts. You delivered the generation of our mortal nature. By your birth you sanctified a virgin's womb. All creation magnifies you, who have manifested yourself among us. You hallowed the streams of Jordan, sending down upon them from heaven your Holy Spirit, and you crushed the heads of the dragons who lurked there.

Wherefore, O King who loves humanity, come now and sanctify this water, by the indwelling of your Holy Spirit.

And grant to it the grace of redemption, the blessing of Jordan. Make it the fountain of incorruption, the gift of sanctification, the remission of sins, the remedy of infirmities, the final destruction of demons, unassailable by hostile powers, filled with angelic might. Let those who would ensnare your creature flee far from it. For we have called upon your name, O Lord, and it is wonderful, and glorious and terrible unto adversaries.

Let all adverse powers be crushed beneath the sign of the image of your cross.

But, O Master of all, show this water to be the water of redemption, the water of sanctification, the purification of flesh and spirit, the loosing of bonds, the remission of sins, the illumination of the soul, the laver of regeneration, the renewal of the Spirit, the gift of adoption, the garment of incorruption, the fountain of life. For you have said, O Lord: Wash and be clean. Put away evil things from your souls. You have bestowed upon us from on high a new birth through water and the Spirit. O Lord, manifest yourself in this water, and grant that those who are baptized here may be transformed; that they may put away from them the old person, which is corrupt through the lusts of the flesh, and that they may be clothed with the new person, and renewed after the image of him who created them: that being buried, after the pattern of your death, in baptism, they may in like manner be partakers of your resurrection; and having preserved the gift of your Holy Spirit, and increased the measure of grace committed to them, they may receive the prize of their high calling, and be numbered with the first-born whose names are written in heaven, in you, our God and Lord, Jesus Christ. For to you are due glory, dominion, honor and worship, together with the Father who is from everlasting, and your all-holy and good and life-giving Spirit, now and ever and unto ages of ages. Amen.

Blessing of water
Orthodox liturgy

FATHER, you give us grace through sacramental signs,
which tell us of the wonders of your
    unseen power.
In baptism we use your gift of water,
  which you have made a rich symbol
  of the grace you give us in this sacrament.
At the very dawn of creation
  your Spirit breathed on the waters,
  making them the wellspring of all holiness.
The waters of the great flood
  you made a sign of the waters of baptism,
  that make an end of sin and a new beginning
    of goodness.
Through the waters of the Red Sea
  you led Israel out of slavery,
  to be an image of God's holy people,
  set free from sin by baptism.
In the waters of the Jordan
  your Son was baptized by John
  and anointed with the Spirit.
Your Son willed that water and blood
  should flow from his side
  as he hung upon the cross.
After his resurrection he told his disciples:
  "Go out and teach all nations,
  baptizing them in the name of the Father
  and of the Son and of the Holy Spirit."
Father, look now with love upon your church,
  and unseal for her the fountain of baptism.
By the power of the Holy Spirit
  give to the water of this font
  the grace of your Son.

You created us in your own likeness:
  cleanse us from sin in a new birth of innocence
  by water and the Spirit.
We ask you, Father, with your Son
  to send the Holy Spirit upon the waters of this font.
May all who are buried with Christ
  in the death of baptism
  rise also with him to newness of life.

*At the words "We ask you, Father" the paschal candle is lowered into the waters and held there until the prayer ends. The prayer is followed by an acclamation with these or other appropriate words:*

Blessing of water
Roman rite

Springs of water, bless the Lord.
Give him glory and praise for ever.

*Presider:*

P RAISE to you, almighty God and Father, for you have created water to cleanse and to give life.

*All:*
Blessed be God.

*Presider:*
Praise to you, Lord Jesus Christ, the Father's only Son, for you offered yourself on the cross, that in the blood and water flowing from your side, and through your death and resurrection, the church might be born.

*All:*
Blessed be God.

*Presider:*
Praise to you, God the Holy Spirit, for you anointed Christ at his baptism in the waters of the Jordan, so that we might all be baptized in you.

*All:*
Blessed be God.

*Presider:*
Come to us, Lord, Father of all, and make holy this water which you have created, so that all who are baptized in it may be washed clean of sin and be born again to live as your children.

*All:*
Hear us, Lord.

*Presider:*
Make this water holy, Lord, so that all who are baptized into Christ's death and resurrection by this water may become more perfectly like your Son.

*All:*
Hear us, Lord.

*The presider touches the water with his right hand and continues.*

Lord, make holy this water which you have created, so that all those whom you have chosen may be born again by the power of the Holy Spirit and may take their place among your holy people.

Blessing of water
Roman rite

B APTISM] is performed with very great simplicity, without pomp, without any large amount of novel preparation, finally, without expense. A person is dipped in water and is sprinkled while some few words are spoken, and then rises again; though not much cleaner, the consequent attainment of eternity is esteemed the more incredible.

Tertullian
Third century

N AME,]
I baptize you in the name of the Father,

*The celebrant immerses the person the first time.*

and of the Son,

*The celebrant immerses the person the second time.*

and of the Holy Spirit.

Rite of baptism
Roman rite

*The celebrant immerses the person the third time.*
*Either or both godparents touch the candidate.*

D ESCEND, Brothers and Sisters marked with the seal,
And put on (Christ) our Lord:
Become yourselves a part of his noble race,
As it is spoken in his parable.

West Syrian
baptismal chants
Fifth century

Stretch out your wings, O holy church,
And greet the simple lambs
whom the Holy Spirit has begotten from the waters.

B LESSED be God
who chose you in Christ.


You are God's work of art, created in Christ Jesus.


You are now God's children, my dearest friends.
What you shall be in his glory has not yet
    been revealed.


Happy are those who have washed their robes clean,
washed in the blood of the Lamb!


You have put on Christ.
In him you have been baptized.
Alleluia, alleluia.

Baptismal acclamations
Roman rite

A WAKE, O sleeper, and arise from the dead,
And Christ shall give you light.

Light of the resurrection,
Begotten before the morning star
Who gives life through his radiance.

*Ancient baptismal acclamation*

Y OU who have been baptized into Christ,
You have put on Christ. Alleluia.
You who have been enlightened in the Father,
In you the Holy Spirit will rejoice. Alleluia.

*Baptismal chant
Armenian rite*

T is not from the well of Jacob,
Nor from the waters made sweet by Moses,
Nor from the river of the Jordan
Which was sanctified by your baptism at the hand
    of John,
But it is from your side, O Christ,
That springs the source of life
Through which our debts are forgiven
And our sins cleansed away.

Chant for procession
to the baptistry
Chaldean rite

IN Baptism—because it is an event—the form and the essence, the "doing" and the "happening," the sign and its meaning coincide, for the purpose of one is precisely to *be* the other, both to reveal and to fulfill it. Baptism *is* what it *represents* because what it represents—death and resurrection—is *true*. It is the representation not of an "idea" but of the very content and reality of the Christian faith itself: to believe in Christ is to "be dead and have one's life hid with him in God" (Col 3:3). Such is the central, overwhelming and all-embracing experience of the early church, an experience so self-evident, so direct, that at first she did not even "explain" it but saw it rather as the source and the condition of all explanations, all theologies.

Alexander Schmemann

B APTISM is the source of "re-membering." It tells us "who we are and who we are becoming," as John the Deacon wrote in the year 500. It tells us that we are the Christ, daily being made more and more into his image. This is dangerous and subversive information. Those who regard human life as worth little are able to countenance any sort of social injustice. Those who know themselves as images of God have a profound sense of dignity and worth born of knowing their divine heritage; and, aware that every other person is also the Christ, they are not satisfied until economic and social structures provide dignity and care for all.

The early church's baptismal liturgy was an experience of social justice, of a new social order, the reign of God. By modeling a new social order, a new creation, in the catechumenate and in baptism, the early church subverted the Roman Empire from within rather than challenging it head on. . . . Christians proclaimed in word and deed that only Jesus, who had accomplished their liberation by his death and resurrection, was the Lord. This undercut allegiance to the Roman imperial system. It is no wonder the Roman Empire persecuted the Christian community. . . .

By choosing voluntarily to forego food, the faithful have made themselves powerless, too. They are ready to stand with the "marginal" of their own community, those called to baptism this Easter. They are thus prepared to discover that, contrary to our society's wisdom, sharing their goods does not deprive them of worth or being; rather, it enables them to be filled with the sense of wholeness and "new creation" that is the heart of the Easter Vigil. This is what the Fathers called "festive fasting." When we choose to be dispossessed of material good, we rediscover it as sacramental; we learn that it is meant to lead us to relationships, not to be an end in itself. . . .

Adult baptism at the Easter Vigil shows the world how God sees the human race. As Nathan Mitchell has noted, the experience of a catechumen in baptism is radically in contrast with the usual experience of interaction in daily life. Where else does one experience being lovingly bathed, massaged with perfumed oil, clothed in a beautiful new garment, embraced, fed, incensed? Yet these are true symbols of the way God sees us; as we act out this love at the Easter Vigil, we reveal the new humanity that God is working to build. . . . Here is a description John Chrysostom gave of a baptismal liturgy at Antioch in the fourth century:

> As soon as the newly baptized come forth from those sacred waters, all who are present embrace them, kiss them, rejoice with them, and congratulate them, because those who were heretofore slaves and captives have suddenly become free men and women and sons and daughters and have been invited to the royal table.

Robert Brooks

T HE ones being baptized] verily die by a symbol of that death which the Quickener of all died; and they surely live with a type of the life without end. Sin and death they put off and cast away in baptism, after the manner of those garments which our Lord departing left in the tomb.

As a babe from the midst of the womb they look forth from the water; and instead of garments the priest receives them and embraces them. They resemble babes when they are lifted up from the midst of the water; and as babes everyone embraces and kisses them. Instead of swaddling clothes they cast garments on their limbs, and adorn them as a bridegroom on the day of the marriage supper.

Narsai
Late fourth century

NAME,] you have become a new creation
and have clothed yourselves in Christ.
Take this white garment
and bring it unstained to the judgment seat of our Lord
    Jesus Christ
Roman rite    so that you may have everlasting life.

BESTOW upon me the shining tunic,
You who are clothed with light as with a mantle,
The Ordo of
Constantinople    Most merciful Christ, our God.

YOU have been enlightened by Christ.
Walk always as children of the light
and keep the flame of faith alive in your hearts.
When the Lord comes, may you go out to meet him
Roman rite    with all the saints in the heavenly kingdom.

O Lord God, who art without generation, and without a superior, the Lord of the whole world, who hast scattered the sweet odor of the knowledge of the gospel among all nations, grant at this time that this chrism may be efficacious upon those that are baptized, that so the sweet odor of thy Christ may continue upon them firm and fixed; and that now they have died with him, they may arise and live with him.

*The Apostolic Constitutions*
Late fourth century

LET us pray, dear friends,
to God, the all-powerful Father,
that he will pour out the Holy Spirit
on these newly baptized
to strengthen them with his abundant gifts
and anoint them to be more like Christ his Son.

All-powerful God, Father of our Lord Jesus Christ,
by water and the Holy Spirit
you freed your sons and daughters from sin
and gave them new life.
Send your Holy Spirit upon them
to be their helper and guide.
Give them the spirit of wisdom and understanding,
the spirit of right judgment and courage,
the spirit of knowledge and reverence.
Fill them with the spirit of wonder and awe in
your presence.

N., be sealed with the Gift of the Holy Spirit.

Laying on of hands
and anointing
Roman rite

GOD of the powers,
Help of all who turn to you
and place themselves under the powerful hand
of your only-begotten Son, we call on you:
By the divine and invisible power
of the Lord and our Savior Jesus Christ,
carry out through this oil your divine and
    heavenly work.

Those who have been baptized receive the anointing,
the impress of the sign of the saving cross
of the only-begotten Son.
By this cross Satan and every hostile power
have been defeated and are led captive
in the triumphal procession.

Regenerated and renewed
by the bath of the new birth,
let these here also share
in the gifts of the Holy Spirit.

Strengthened by the seal,
let them remain "steadfast and immovable"
sheltered from all attack and pillaging,
subjected neither to insult nor to aggression.
Let them live to the very end in faith and
    the knowledge of the truth,
in expectation of the hope of heavenly life
and of the eternal promises
of the Lord and our Savior Jesus Christ.
Through him, glory to you and power,
in the Holy Spirit,

Serapion
Fourth century    now and for ever and ever. Amen.

D EAR friends,
through the paschal mystery
we have been buried with Christ in baptism,
so that we may rise with him to a new life.
Now that we have completed our lenten observance,
let us renew the promises we made in baptism
when we rejected Satan and his works,
and promised to serve God faithfully
in his holy Catholic church.                    Roman rite

D O you reaffirm your renunciation of evil and renew your commitment to Jesus Christ?

*The following are added to the usual promises.*

Will you continue in the apostles' teaching and
  fellowship in the breaking of bread,
  and in the prayers?
I will, with God's help.

Will you persevere in resisting evil, and, whenever you
  fall into sin, repent and return to the Lord?
I will, with God's help.

Will you proclaim by word and example the good news
  of God in Christ?
I will, with God's help.

Will you seek and serve Christ in all persons, loving
  your neighbor as yourself?
I will, with God's help.

Will you strive for justice and peace among all people
  and respect the dignity of every human being?
I will, with God's help.

May almighty God, the Father of our Lord Jesus Christ,
who has given us a new birth by water and the Holy Spirit,
and bestowed upon us the forgiveness of sins, keep us in
eternal life by his grace, in Christ Jesus our Lord. Amen.

*The Book of Common Prayer*

I N peace,
let us pray to the Lord.

For peace from on high and for the salvation of our souls . . .

That the Lord Jesus Christ, our Savior, may grant us triumph and victory over the temptations of our visible and invisible enemies . . .

That we may crush beneath our feet the Prince of Darkness and his powers . . .

That he may raise us with him and make us rise from the tomb of our sins and offenses . . .

That he may fill us with the joy and happiness of his holy resurrection . . .

That we may deserve the grace of entering into the chamber of his divine wedding-feast and rejoice beyond limit, together with his heavenly attendants and the hosts of saints glorified through him in the church triumphant in heaven . . .

Help us, save us, have mercy on us, and protect us, O God, by your grace.

Let us remember our all-holy, spotless, most highly blessed and glorious Lady and Mother of God and ever-virgin Mary, with all the saints, and commend ourselves and one another and our whole life to Christ our God.

For you are our Light and our Resurrection, O Christ our God, and we send up glory to you and to your eternal Father and to your all-holy, good and life-giving Spirit, now and always and for ever and ever.

Easter Sunday
Orthodox liturgy

FATHER, all-powerful and ever-living God,
we do well always and everywhere to give
    you thanks
through Jesus Christ our Lord.
We praise you with greater joy than ever
on this Easter night,
when Christ became our paschal sacrifice.
He is the true Lamb who took away the sins
    of the world.

Preface
Roman rite

By dying he destroyed our death;
by rising he restored our life.

BAPTISM is inadequately perceptible apart from the
eucharist; the eucharist is not wholly knowable
without reference to conversion in faith; conversion is
abortive if it does not issue in sacramental illumination by
incorporation into the church; the church is only an inept
corporation without steady access to Sunday, Lent, and
the Easter Vigil; evangelization is mere noise and
catechesis only a syllabus apart from conversion and
initiation into a robust ecclesial environment of faith
shared. In baptism the eucharist begins, and in the
eucharist baptism is sustained. From this premier

Aidan Kavanagh    sacramental union flows all the church's life.

D RAW near and take the body of the Lord,
And drink with faith the blood
for you outpoured.

Saved by his body, hallowed by his blood,
   With souls refreshed we render thanks to God.

Salvation's giver, Christ, the only Son,
   By his dear cross and blood the vict'ry won.

He, ransomer from death and light from shade,
   Now gives his holy grace his saints to aid.

Let us approach with faithful hearts sincere,
   And take the pledges of salvation here.

The Lord in this world rules his saints, and shields,
   To all believers life eternal yields:

With heav'nly bread makes those who hunger whole,
   Gives living waters to the thirsting soul.

Before your presence, Lord, all people bow.
   In this your feast of love be with us now.

Latin hymn
Seventh century

THERE *flowed from his side water and blood.* Beloved, do not pass over this mystery without thought; it has yet another hidden meaning, which I will explain to you. I said that water and blood symbolized baptism and the holy eucharist. From these two sacraments the church is born: from baptism, *the cleansing water that gives rebirth and renewal through the Holy Spirit,* and from the holy eucharist. Since the symbols of baptism and the eucharist flowed from his side, it was from his side that Christ fashioned the church, as he had fashioned Eve from the side of Adam. Moses give a hint of this when he tells the story of the first man and makes him exclaim: *Bone from my bones and flesh from my flesh!* As God then took a rib from Adam's side to fashion a woman, so Christ has given us blood and water from his side to fashion the church. God took the rib when Adam was in a deep sleep, and in the same way Christ gave us the blood and the water after his own death.

Do you understand, then, how Christ has united his bride to himself and what food he gives us all to eat? By one and the same food we are both brought into being and nourished. As a woman nourishes her child with her own blood and milk, so does Christ unceasingly nourish with his own blood those to whom he himself has given life.

John Chrysostom
Fifth century
Liturgy of the Hours
Roman rite

THIS holy and blessed day is the first of the week, the king and master of all days, the feast of feasts and the season of seasons. On this day we bless Christ for ever and ever.

O faithful, come on this day of the glorious resurrection: let us drink the wine of the new vineyard, of the divine joy, of the kingdom of Christ! Let us praise him as our God for ever and ever.

Easter Sunday
Orthodox liturgy

THIS is the day the Lord has made; let us rejoice and be glad, alleluia.

Very early on the morning after the Sabbath, when the sun had just risen, they came to the tomb, alleluia.

Liturgy of the Hours
Roman rite

CHRISTIANS, praise the paschal victim!
Offer thankful sacrifice!

Christ the lamb has saved the sheep,
Christ the just one paid the price,
Reconciling sinners to the Father.

Death and life fought bitterly
For this wondrous victory;
The Lord of life who died reigns glorified!

O Mary, come and say
what you saw at break of day.

"The empty tomb of my living Lord!
I saw Christ Jesus risen and adored!

"Bright angels testified,
Shroud and grave clothes side by side!

"Yes, Christ my hope rose gloriously.
He goes before you into Galilee."

Share the good news, sing joyfully:
His death is victory!
Lord Jesus, victor King,
Show us mercy. Amen.

Easter sequence
Roman rite
Eleventh century

I am a flower of Sharon,
　a lily of the valley.

As a lily among thorns,
　so is my beloved among women.

As an apple tree among the trees of the woods,
　so is my lover among men.

I delight to rest in his shadow,
　and his fruit is sweet to my mouth.
He brings me into the banquet hall
　and his emblem over me is love.
Strengthen me with raisin cakes,
　refresh me with apples,
　for I am faint with love.
His left hand is under my head
　and his right arm embraces me.
I adjure you, daughters of Jerusalem,
　by the gazelles and hinds of the field,
Do not arouse, do not stir up love
　before its own time.

Hark! my lover—here he comes
　springing across the mountains,
　leaping across the hills.
My lover is like a gazelle
　or a young stag.
Here he stands behind our wall,
　gazing through the windows,
　peering through the lattices.
My lover speaks; he says to me,
　"Arise, my beloved, my beautiful one,
　and come!
For see, the winter is past,
　the rains are over and gone.

The flowers appear on the earth,
  the time of pruning the vines has come,
  and the song of the dove is heard in our land.
The fig tree puts forth its figs,
  and the vines, in bloom, give forth fragrance.
Arise, my beloved, my beautiful one,
  and come!''

Song of Songs
2:1–13

COME, ye faithful, raise the strain
Of triumphant gladness!
God has brought his Israel
Into joy from sadness:
Loosed from Pharaoh's bitter yoke
Jacob's sons and daughters,
Led them with unmoistened foot
Through the Red Sea waters.

'Tis the spring of souls today:
Christ hath burst his prison;
And from three days' sleep in death
As a sun has risen.
All the winter of our sins,
Long and dark, is flying
From his light, to whom we give
Laud and praise undying.

Now the queen of seasons bright
With the day of splendor,
With the royal feast of feasts,
Comes its joy to render:
Come to glad Jerusalem,
Who with true affection
Welcomes, in unwearied strains,
Jesus' resurrection.

John of Damascus
Eighth century

ALLELUIA!
Alleluia!

When Israel came forth from Egypt,
Jacob's children from an alien people,
Judah became the Lord's temple,
Israel became his kingdom.

The sea fled at the sight:
the Jordan turned back on its course,
the mountains leapt like rams
and the hills like yearling sheep.

Why was it, sea, that you fled,
that you turned back, Jordan, in your course?
Mountains, that you leapt like rams,
hills, like yearling sheep?

Tremble, O earth, before the Lord,
in the presence of the God of Jacob,
who turns the rock into a pool
and flint into a spring of water.                    Psalm 114

L IGHT'S glittering morn bedecks the sky,
 Heaven thunders forth its victor cry;
The glad earth shouts its triumph high,
And groaning hell makes wild reply.

While he the King of glorious might
Treads down death's strength in death's despite,
And trampling hell by victor's right,
Brings forth his sleeping saints to light.

Hell's pains are loosed, and tears are fled;
Captivity is captive led;
The angel, crowned with light, has said,
"The Lord is risen from the dead."

We pray thee, King with glory decked,
In this our paschal joy, protect
From all that death would fain affect
Thy ransomed flock, thine own elect.

Latin hymn
Fifth century

N OW that we have seen the resurrection of Christ, let
 us adore the all-holy Lord Jesus, the only sinless one.
We bow in worship before your cross, O Christ, and we
praise and glorify your resurrection, for you are our God,
and we have no other, and we magnify your name. All
you faithful, come: let us adore the holy resurrection of
Christ, for, behold, through the cross joy has come to the
world! Let us always bless the Lord, let us sing his
resurrection, for by enduring for us the pain of the cross,
he has crushed death by his death.

Easter Sunday
Orthodox liturgy

CHRIST Jesus lay in death's strong bonds
For our offences given;
But now at God's right hand he stands
And brings us light from heaven.
Wherefore let us joyful be
And sing to God right thankfully
Loud songs of Hallelujah! Hallelujah!

It was a strange and dreadful strife
When life and death contended;
The victory remained with life,
The reign of death was ended;
Stript of power, no more he reigns,
An empty form alone remains;
His sting is lost for ever. Hallelujah!

So let us keep the festival
Whereto the Lord invites us;
Christ is himself the joy of all,
The sun that warms and lights us;
By his grace he doth impart
Eternal sunshine to the heart;
The night of sin is ended. Hallelujah!

Then let us feast this Easter day
On the true bread of heaven.
The word of grace hath purged away
The old and wicked leaven.
Christ alone our souls will feed,
He is our meat and drink indeed,
Faith lives upon no other. Hallelujah!

Martin Luther
Sixteenth century

HAIL thee, festival day!
Blest day to be hallowed forever;
Day when our Lord was raised, breaking the kingdom
    of death.

All the fair beauty of earth from the death of
    the winter arising!
Ev'ry good gift of the year now with its master returns.

Rise from the grave now, O Lord, the author of life
    and creation.
Treading the pathway of death, new life you give
    to us all.

God the Almighty, the Lord, the ruler of earth
    and the heavens,
Guard us from harm without; cleanse us from evil
    within.

Jesus, the health of the world, enlighten our minds,
    great Redeemer,
Son of the Father supreme, only begotten of God.

Spirit of life and of power, now flow in us,
    fount of our being,
Light that enlightens us all, life that in all may abide.

Praise to the giver of good! O Lover and Author
    of concord,
Pour out your balm on our days; order our ways
    in your peace.

Fortunatus
Sixth century

L ET God arise and his enemies will scatter, and those who hate him will flee before him.

Our passover, Christ the redeemer is revealed to us today as a noble Passover. It is a new and holy Passover, a mystical Passover, a blameless Passover, a glorious Passover, a Passover for the faithful, a Passover that opens for us the gates of paradise, a Passover that sanctifies all believers.

A glorious Passover has shown upon us, a Passover of the Lord, a Passover perfectly honorable: let us then embrace one another with joy. O what a Passover delivering from sorrow, for Christ coming out of the tomb as from a nuptial chamber fills the women with joy by telling them to bring this happy news to the disciples.

Behold, today is the day of the resurrection: let us glory in the feast, let us embrace one another in joy and say: "O friends and enemies too: we forgive everything on resurrection day. Let us all sing together: Christ is risen from the dead!"

Christ is risen!

He is truly risen!

Easter Sunday
Orthodox liturgy

# Paschal Vespers

### History
Paschal vespers, in the sense of its celebration suggested in the *General Instruction on the Liturgy of the Hours, #213,* is rooted in the Roman church's practice of going in procession from the basilica to the baptistry at St. John Lateran (the cathedral church of Rome) on Easter Sunday evening. This practice continued for centuries in Rome and was adopted by many cathedral churches of Europe, but declined as adult initiation became infrequent. A few cathedrals and some religious orders retained this special paschal vespers to the present day and at least one diocese has revived the practice in a renewed form.

The celebration of paschal vespers enables a community to close the Triduum by again making contact with those symbols which speak to the initiatory practice: the newly baptized in the midst of the assembly, the font, the paschal candle.

### An Overview
The central signs of vespers—the paschal candle and the incense along with the additional sign of the Easter mystery, the water/baptismal font—are given special attention during the celebration of Easter vespers. If at all possible, these signs should be located in separate places to which the assembly moves in body and not just in sight and spirit. However, the arrangement should not be radically different from that of the Vigil since the use of a common setting gives unity to the celebration of the Easter mystery in its separate moments.

It is recommended therefore that:
1. The people assemble in an area from which they can easily move (for instance, the church lobby or an adjacent meeting room or parlor). Avoid any place with chairs or pews which must be navigated around.
2. The Easter candle, which has been burning all day long, be in a prominent place. For this occasion, at

least, the assembly moves into the presence of the light, rather than the light coming into its midst. The space around the candle should be large enough for the assembly to gather without too much crowding.

3. An incense brazier (preferably not a thurible) be in a fixed place, again with sufficient space for the assembly to gather.
4. The baptismal font, rather than the place where the Easter water was blessed, be the place for the last part of the liturgy. This is the place of our new birth.
5. The normative posture for this liturgy be standing and moving.
6. The people be given only a card with the hymn text and appropriate refrains.

The above description is of the ideal setting for this liturgy. An adaptation which requires the movement of the entire assembly is the minimum expectation.

**The Movement of the Liturgy**
The people assemble in the appropriate area. When it is time, the celebrant, an assistant and a thurifer carrying a lighted and smoking thurible join them.

*I. The Light Service.* The hymn to the light is begun, during which all move to the place where the Easter candle stands. For ease of movement it is suggested that the presider, assistant and thurifer lead the procession.

The Easter candle is generously incensed by the presider when they arrive at the candle while the rest of the assembly gathers.

The thanksgiving prayer is intoned by the presider. At the conclusion of the thanksgiving prayer all move without ceremony to the place where the incense rite is to be held. An invitation such as "Let us pray for pardon, peace and protection," or "Let us pray for unity and peace in God's service," or some variant appropriate to the Easter season might be spoken as a signal to move. The thurible is left near the paschal candle.

*II. The Incense Rite.* When all arrive at the place for the incense rite, the presider places a generous amount of incense on the coals in the brazier. As the smoke begins to rise the cantor begins the antiphon to the incense psalm (Psalm 141: "I have called to you, O Lord") and sings the psalm. The people repeat the refrain between the verses. A more joyful melody than that used during the season of Lent is recommended. The placing of incense on the coals of the brazier is preferable to a general incensing of the assembly partly because of the clearer allusion to the Temple sacrifice of incense, but also because the action using the thurible is more of an honorific sign and the rite here is penitential. A prayer concludes this rite.

*III. The Service at the Font.* The procession to the font is accompanied by either the Canticle of Mary (the Magnificat) or Psalm 114, "When Israel came forth from Egypt." An alleluia is a suitable response to both of these. When all arrive at the font, the general intercessions are sung. These are followed by the Lord's Prayer, a sprinkling with water from the font and the kiss of peace. In both the general intercessions and the kiss of peace the neophytes should be given due regard. The liturgy closes with a blessing and a dismissal with an alleluia.

# I. The Light Service

*Presider:*
Jesus Christ is the Light of the world.
*All:*
A Light no darkness can overpower.

## Hymn

*At the present time there seems to be no hymn that incorporates both the theme of light-evening and the Easter mystery of dying and rising in baptism. Such a hymn would be ideal. The hymn, "Come, you faithful raise the strain," comes close. The model hymn that deals with light-evening is "O Radiant Light" (as translated by William Storey, it is available from LTP in* Evening Prayer: The Leader's Book).

## Thanksgiving Prayer

Blessed are you, O Lord our God.
In every age you have written our history in water.
From the chaos of the seas you brought forth our world.
From the midst of the Red Sea you gave birth
    to a people.
Through the Jordan you brought Israel
    to a promised land
and sent forth your Son to be the anointed
who would proclaim the good news of your kingdom.
In these days you have again recreated and formed us.
In the memorial of Christ's death and rising
new sons and daughters have been born
from the font, the womb of your church.
Keep alive in all of us the joy of this season
that always and everywhere the Easter alleluia
may arise as a hymn of glory to your name.
All power and glory be to you
through Jesus our risen Lord
in the life-giving love of the Holy Spirit
this eventide and for ever and ever.
Amen.

# II. The Incense Rite

## Invitation (optional)

Let us pray for unity and peace in God's service.
Let us pray for pardon, peace and protection.

## Incense psalm

*Psalm 141 is used. The refrain should be based on the second verse of the psalm: "Let my prayer come like incense before you, the lifting up of my hands, like the evening sacrifice." Musical settings for this can be found in* Evening Prayer, The Leader's Book *(LTP) or* Praise God in Song *(GIA). One should remember that there is a joyful character to the entire service and this psalm and rite should not be an exception.*

## Collect

Accept, O God, our creator,
this evening sacrifice
which rises to you from hearts renewed
by the celebration of the Easter mysteries.
Lead all your people
to that paschal banquet
where we shall rejoice in unity of heart and mind.
Amen.

# III. The Service at the Font

## Procession to the font

*During the procession the Magnificat or Psalm 114 should be sung. The Magnificat praises God for the marvelous deeds he has done for us, while the psalm reminds us of the new life we have received from God in our deliverance from Egypt. Many settings for the Magnificat exist. The festal setting in the Gelineau version is excellent because of the alleluia refrain. There is also a Gelineau setting for Psalm 114 (113A in the Gelineau numbering).*

## General intercessions

*The general intercessions should be as they are labeled— general intercessions for the church. The season should be taken into account and so should the unique character of this vesper service. The neophytes should be prayed for along with the commemoration of the new life of all believers. Models for these intercessions can be found in* Morning Praise *and* Evensong *(Fides) and* Praise God in Song *(GIA) in the supplementary sections.*

## The Lord's Prayer

*Many musical settings of this can be found.*

## The sprinkling with baptismal water

*This sprinkling should be generous, and since the assembly will probably be rather small there is no reason why everyone should not get wet. An evergreen branch is a fitting aspergil.*

## The kiss of peace

*Be sure to greet the neophytes!*

## Solemn blessing and dismissal

*A solemn, joyful form should be used for both and should include an alleluia.*

*The model of paschal vespers suggested here might be used not only on Easter Sunday, but on all of the Sundays of the Easter season.*

Alan Scheible
Laurence Mayer
Andrew Ciferni

BLESSED are you, O Lord almighty
who illumine the day with the brightness of the sun
and delight the night with the glow of fire,
who have made us worthy to live through
    this whole day
and come close to the night.
Hear our prayers and those of all your people;
forgive us our sins, both deliberate and indeliberate
and accept our evening petition;
send down upon your inheritance
the riches of your mercy and compassion;
surround us with your holy angels;
cover us with the armor of your justice;
keep us in the ways of your righteousness;
protect us with your power
against any harm or conspiracy of the devil;
grant us that this evening, and the approaching night,
and all the days of our life,
may be perfect, holy, peaceful, without sin,
without stumbling or vain imagination,
through the intercession of the Mother of God
and of all the saints

Evening prayer
Orthodox liturgy    who ever pleased you since time began. Amen.

# Notes

## Triduum

THE CHURCH: *The Orthodox Faith*, vol. 2, *Worship* by Thomas Hopko © 1972 Department of Religious Education, The Orthodox Church in America. Reprinted with permission.

AND LET: "Apostolic Tradition of Hippolytus," ed. Dom Gregory Dix, from *Documents of the Baptismal Liturgy*, 2d ed. © 1960, 1970 E. C. Whitaker. Published by SPCK, London. Reprinted with permission.

CHRIST REDEEMED: General Norms for the Liturgical Year, #18–21, *The Roman Calendar*.

EVEN THOUGH: *Great Lent* by Alexander Schmemann, © 1969 St. Vladimir's Seminary Press. Reprinted with permission.

THIS IS: *Early Christian Prayers*, ed. A. Hamman, trans. by Walter Mitchell, English translation © 1961 Longmans, Green and Co. Ltd. Reprinted with permission of Regnery Gateway, Inc.

## Holy Thursday

SING, MY: "Pange lingua gloriosi proelium," composite translation.

LET ALL: *Orthodox Hymns* by Alexander A. Bogolepov, © 1976 St. Vladimir's Seminary Press. Reprinted with permission.

BUT IMITATE: Translation by Agnes Cunningham.

WE PROCLAIM: Translation by Agnes Cunningham.

JESUS, COME: From "A Homily on Isaiah 5:2," translation by Agnes Cunningham.

FELLOW SERVANTS: "At the Foot-Washing" from *The Book of Occasional Services*, © 1979 The Church Pension Fund.

OF THY: As quoted in *The Orthodox Faith*, vol. 2, *Worship* by Thomas Hopko, ©1972 Department of Religious Education, The Orthodox Church in America. Reprinted with permission.

TO KNOW: *The Shape of Baptism: The Rite of Christian Initiation* by Aidan Kavanagh, © 1978 Pueblo Publishing Company, Inc. Reprinted with permission.

THOU WHO: *Orthodox Hymns* by Alexander A. Bogolepov, © 1976 St. Vladimir's Seminary Press. Reprinted with permission.

HAIL OUR: "Pange lingua gloriosi corporis" from *New Hymns for All Seasons*, © 1969 James Quinn. Printed by permission of Geoffrey Chapman, a division of Cassell Ltd.

## Good Friday

LET THE: *Constitution on the Sacred Liturgy*, #110, published by the National Catholic Welfare Conference, Washington DC.

IT IS: *I Loved This People* by Dietrich Bonhoeffer, © 1965, used by permission of John Knox Press, Atlanta.

LET US: Reprinted from *Kontakia of Romanos, Byzantine Melodist*, trans. Marjorie Carpenter, by permission of the University of Missouri Press, © 1970 by the Curators of the University of Missouri.

WEARY OF ALL TRUMPETING: by Martin Franzmann, © 1971. Reprinted with permission of Chantry Music Press, Inc.

YOU LOVE: Translation by Agnes Cunningham.

ST. JOHN: *The Liturgical Year*, vol. 3, by Adrian Nocent, published by The Liturgical Press. Copyrighted by The Order of St. Benedict, Inc., Collegeville MN.

IN NEW TESTAMENT: "Israel as Warp and Woof in John's Gospel" by Gerard Sloyan, *Face to Face: An Interreligious Bulletin*, winter and spring 1982. Published by the Anti-Defamation League of B'nai B'rith.

PETER, APOSTLE: "Mary's Keen" from *Caoineadh na Maighdine* published by Gael-Linn, Cliath, Ireland.

JOSEPH WENT: *Byzantine Daily Worship*, © 1969. Quoted with permission of Alleluia Press, Allendale NJ.

BROTHERS AND: Three to five individuals speak the invocations. The cantor voices the final petition in each group, cueing the response of the whole community with the words, "Let us pray to the Lord." After the assembly's response and an interval of silence, the presider sings or speaks the prayer.

If desired, and if the movement can easily be done, the presider and people can kneel for the silence and the prayer. The refrain that is sung by all, either the one given here or another that is suitable, should be familiar so that everyone will join in. A simple "Lord, hear our prayer" would be better than an assembly fumbling with papers: the alertness of the particular group to direction would be the governing consideration.

It is best to avoid typecasting in selecting people to speak particular petitions. There should be male, female, young, old voices, but it would be less desirable to have, say, children praying for children and old people for old people than to have persons who are, in their own lives, especially concerned with a special group praying for that group.

**I AM:** In this prayer, the repetition of the brief scripture passage and the constant repetition of the assembly's refrain, breaking up the presider's petitions, can create a strong ritual. The use of music is important. The scriptural passage could be sung or spoken. The presider's words could also be spoken, but the assembly's words should be sung to a simple melody. It is a litany prayer and should have that feeling. If the presider's words are not sung, a very sparse instrumental accompaniment may serve to cue and sustain the refrain.

**BECAUSE FOR:** *Early Christian Prayers,* ed. A. Hamman, trans. by Walter Mitchell, English translation © 1961 Longmans, Green and Co. Ltd. Reprinted by permission of Regnery Gateway, Inc.

**THE ROYAL:** "Vexilla Regis," verses 4, 5 from *The Hymnal 1940* © The Church Pension Fund 1940, 1943, 1961; verse 6 from *The Catholic Liturgy Book* © 1975 Romda Ltd.

**BY THE CROSS:** "Images of the Cross," trans. Fred Pratt Green, from *The Hymns and Ballads of Fred Pratt Green,* © 1974 by Hope Publishing Co., Carol Stream IL 60187. All rights reserved. Used by permission.

**O HEAVEN:** Reprinted from *Kontakia of Romanos, Byzantine Melodist,* translated by Marjorie Carpenter, by permission of the University of Missouri Press, © 1970 by the Curators of the University of Missouri.

## Holy Saturday

**O FAITHFUL:** *Byzantine Daily Worship,* © 1969. Quoted with permission of Alleluia Press, Allendale NJ.

**THE ELECT:** *Rite of Christian Initiation of Adults* (RCIA), #26.

**TODAY HADES:** *Byzantine Daily Worship,* © 1969. Quoted with permission of Alleluia Press, Allendale NJ.

**O CHRIST:** *Orthodox Hymns* by Alexander A. Bogolepov, © 1976 St. Vladimir's Seminary Press. Reprinted with permission.

**THE DEVIL:** Reprinted from *Kontakia of Romanos, Byzantine Melodist,* trans. Marjorie Carpenter, by permission of the University of Missouri Press, © 1970 by the Curators of the University of Missouri.

**O LORD:** *Orthodox Hymns* by Alexander A. Bogolepov, © 1976 St. Valdimir's Seminary Press. Reprinted with permission.

**SING HYMNS:** Reprinted from *Kontakia of Romanos, Byzantine Melodist,* trans. Marjorie Carpenter, by permission of the University of Missouri Press, © 1970 by the Curators of the University of Missouri.

## Keeping Vigil

**WE, BELOVED:** *Early Christian Prayers,* ed. A. Hamman, trans. by Walter Mitchell, English translation © 1961 Longmans, Green and Co. Ltd. Reprinted by permission of Regnery Gateway, Inc.

**NOW, O LORD:** *Byzantine Daily Worship,* © 1969. Quoted with permission of Alleluia Press, Allendale NJ.

**COME, O FAITHFUL:** *Byzantine Daily Worship,* © 1969. Quoted with permission of Alleluia Press, Allendale NJ.

**O NIGHT:** *Early Christian Prayers,* ed. A. Hamman, trans. by Walter Mitchell, English translation © 1961 Longmans, Green and Co. Ltd. Reprinted by permission of Regnery Gateway, Inc.

THIS IS: *Early Christian Prayers,* ed. A. Hamman, trans. by Walter Mitchell, English translation © 1961 Longmans, Green and Co. Ltd. Reprinted by permission of Regnery Gateway, Inc.

O GOD, BY THE: Reprinted from *Lutheran Book of Worship: Minister's Desk Edition,* © 1978 by permission of Augsburg Publishing House.

O GOD, YOU HAVE UNITED: Reprinted from *Lutheran Book of Worship: Minister's Desk Edition,* © 1978 by permission of Augsburg Publishing House.

LET US: *The Paschal Mystery,* ed. A. Hamman, © 1969. Reprinted with the permission of Alba House Publications

AFTER THE: In the Byzantine tradition the gospel is Matthew 28:1–20, but this tradition also knows the reading of Mark 16:1–18 and of John 1:1–17. Matthew 28:1–10 is the selection of *The Book of Common Prayer.* Matthew 28:1–7 was the Vigil gospel of the Roman rite before the reform of the lectionary.

LET ALL: Adapted from *Byzantine Daily Worship,* © 1969. Reprinted with permission of Alleluia Press, Allendale NJ.

IT IS: Translation by Frank Quinn.

CHRISTES PEPULL: *Mirk's Festival* by John Mirk, London, 1905.

THE TEXT: *The Paschal Mystery,* ed. A. Hamman, © 1969. Reprinted with the permission of Alba House Publications.

## Initiation

THE WATER: *Springtime of the Liturgy* by Lucien Deiss, published by The Liturgical Press. Copyrighted by The Order of St. Benedict, Inc., Collegeville MN.

THEN THE: RCIA, #214.

DO YOU REJECT: RCIA, #217, 219.

THE RENUNCIATION: *The Sacramental Mysteries: A Byzantine Approach* by Casimir A. Kucharek, © 1976. Quoted with permission of Alleluia Press, Allendale NJ.

DO YOU: From *Service Book of the Holy Orthodox-Catholic Apostolic Church,* © 1975 by permission of the Antiochian Orthodox Christian Archdiocese of North America.

TO RENOUNCE: *Of Water and the Spirit* by Alexander Schmemann, © 1974 St. Vladimir's Seminary Press. Reprinted with permission.

DEAR AND: *Springtime of the Liturgy* by Lucien Deiss, published by The Liturgical Press. Copyrighted by The Order of St. Benedict, Inc., Collegeville MN.

A THREEFOLD: *The Sacramental Mysteries: A Byzantine Approach* by Casimir A. Kucharek, © 1976. Quoted with permission of Alleluia Press, Allendale NJ.

BAPTISM'S KNOWLEDGE: *The Shape of Baptism: The Rite of Christain Initiation* by Aidan Kavanagh, © 1978 Pueblo Publishing Company, Inc. Reprinted with permission.

O MASTER: *Springtime of the Liturgy* by Lucien Deiss, published by The Liturgical Press. Copyrighted by The Order of St. Benedict, Inc., Collegeville MN.

FROM THIS: *Springtime of the Liturgy* by Lucien Deiss, published by The Liturgical Press. Copyrighted by The Order of St. Benedict, Inc., Collegeville MN.

THE BROOD: *Early Christian Prayers,* ed. A. Hamman, trans. by Walter Mitchell, English translation © 1961 Longmans, Green and Co. Ltd. Reprinted by permission of Regnery Gateway, Inc.

ETERNAL LORD: Translation by Agnes Cunningham.

KING AND: *Springtime of the Liturgy* by Lucien Deiss, published by The Liturgical Press. Copyrighted by The Order of St. Benedict, Inc., Collegeville MN.

GREAT ARE: *Service Book of the Holy Orthodox-Catholic Apostolic Church,* © 1975 by permission of the Antiochian Orthodox Christian Archdiocese of North America.

FATHER, YOU: RCIA, #215.

PRAISE TO: RCIA, #389.

**BAPTISM IS PERFORMED:** As quoted in *The Sacramental Mysteries: A Byzantine Approach* by Casimir A. Kucharek, © 1976. Quoted with permission of Alleluia Press, Allendale NJ.

**NAME, I BAPTIZE:** RCIA, #220.

**DESCEND, BROTHERS:** As quoted in "The Chants of the Baptismal Liturgy" by Joseph Gelineau, *Adult Baptism and the Catechumenate,* Concilium vol. 22, © 1967 by Paulist Fathers, Inc. and Stichting Concilium. Reprinted with permission.

**BLESSED BE:** RCIA, #390.

**AWAKE, O SLEEPER:** Ephesians 5:14 is "the most ancient Christian baptismal hymn." We know how the hymn continued from a quotation by Clement of Alexandria.

As quoted by Joseph Gelineau in *Adult Baptism and the Catechumenate,* Concilium vol. 22, © 1967 by Paulist Fathers, Inc. and Stichting Concilium. Reprinted by permission.

**YOU WHO:** Variations of this chant are found in the Byzantine, Chaldean, Mozarabic and Roman rites.

As quoted by Joseph Gelineau in *Adult Baptism and the Catechumenate,* Concilium vol. 22, © 1967 by Paulist Fathers, Inc. and Stichting Concilium. Reprinted by permission.

**IT IS:** As quoted by Joseph Gelineau in *Adult Baptism and the Catechumenate,* Concilium vol. 22, © 1967 by Paulist Fathers, Inc. and Stichting Concilium. Reprinted by permission.

**IN BAPTISM:** *Of Water and the Spirit* by Alexander Schmemann, © 1974, St. Vladimir's Seminary Press. Reprinted with permission.

**BAPTISM IS:** "The Great Feast, Font of Justice," by Robert Brooks, *Liturgy: Feasts and Fasting,* © The Liturgical Conference, 810 Rhode Island Ave. NE, Washington DC 20018. Used with permission. All rights reserved.

**THE ONES:** *The Liturgical Homilies of Narsai,* ed. R. H. Connolly. Cambridge University Publications.

**NAME, YOU HAVE:** RCIA, #225.

**BESTOW UPON:** As quoted by Joseph Gelineau in *Adult Baptism and the Catechumenate,* Concilium vol. 22, © 1967 by Paulist Fathers, Inc. and Stichting Concilium. Reprinted with permission.

**YOU HAVE BEEN:** RCIA, #226.

**O LORD:** "Didascalia et Constitutiones Apostolorum," trans. F. X. Funk, from *Documents of the Baptismal Liturgy,* 2d ed., © 1960, 1970 E. C. Whitaker. Published by SPCK, London. Reprinted with permission.

**LET US PRAY:** RCIA, #229–230, 231.

**GOD OF:** *Springtime of the Liturgy* by Lucien Deiss, published by The Liturgical Press. Copyrighted by The Order of St. Benedict, Inc., Collegeville MN.

**IN PEACE:** *Byzantine Daily Worship,* © 1969. Quoted with permission of Alleluia Press, Allendale NJ.

**BAPTISM IS INADEQUATELY:** *The Shape of Baptism: The Rite of Christian Initiation* by Aidan Kavanagh, © 1978 Pueblo Publishing Company, Inc. Reprinted with permission.

**DRAW NEAR:** Translation by John Mason Neale, alt.

## Easter

**THIS HOLY:** *Byzantine Daily Worship,* © 1969. Quoted with permission of Alleluia Press, Allendale NJ.

**CHRISTIANS, PRAISE:** Attributed to Wipo of Burgundy. Translation by Peter Scagnelli.

**COME, YE:** Translation by John Mason Neale, alt.

**LIGHT'S GLITTERING:** Attributed to Ambrose. Translation by John Mason Neale.

**NOW THAT:** *Byzantine Daily Worship,* © 1969. Quoted with permission of Alleluia Press, Allendale NJ.

**CHRIST JESUS:** Translation by Richard Massie.

**HAIL THEE:** Reprinted from *Lutheran Book of Worship,* © 1978 by permission of Augsburg Publishing House.

**LET GOD:** *Byzantine Daily Worship,* © 1969. Quoted with permission of Alleluia Press, Allendale NJ.

**BLESSED ARE:** *Byzantine Daily Worship,* © 1969. Quoted with permission of Alleluia Press, Allendale NJ.